Civil Society and Activism in the Middle East

Civil Society and Activism in the Middle East

Regime Breakdown vs. Regime Continuity

Nadine Sika

OXFORD
UNIVERSITY PRESS

Great Clarendon Street, Oxford, OX2 6DP,
United Kingdom

Oxford University Press is a department of the University of Oxford.
It furthers the University's objective of excellence in research, scholarship,
and education by publishing worldwide. Oxford is a registered trade mark of
Oxford University Press in the UK and in certain other countries

© Nadine Sika 2024

The moral rights of the author have been asserted

All rights reserved. No part of this publication may be reproduced, stored in
a retrieval system, or transmitted, in any form or by any means, without the
prior permission in writing of Oxford University Press, or as expressly permitted
by law, by licence or under terms agreed with the appropriate reprographics
rights organization. Enquiries concerning reproduction outside the scope of the
above should be sent to the Rights Department, Oxford University Press, at the
address above

You must not circulate this work in any other form
and you must impose this same condition on any acquirer

Published in the United States of America by Oxford University Press
198 Madison Avenue, New York, NY 10016, United States of America

British Library Cataloguing in Publication Data

Data available

Library of Congress Control Number: 2023946227

ISBN 9780198882411

DOI: 10.1093/oso/9780198882411.001.0001

Printed and bound by
CPI Group (UK) Ltd, Croydon, CR0 4YY

Links to third party websites are provided by Oxford in good faith and
for information only. Oxford disclaims any responsibility for the materials
contained in any third party website referenced in this work.

To Celine, Tamer and Edward

Acknowledgements

Writing this book was an interesting journey for which I am indebted to many colleagues, friends and family. I am most thankful to all civil society actors in Jordan and in Egypt who accepted to be part of our research project through giving us time for interviews, focus groups, and expert opinions. This book was part of a larger research project that was generously funded by the Carnegie Corporation New York. My partner in this research project was Dr. Aida Essaid, former director of the Information and Research Center, King Hussein Foundation. She led the research team in Jordan, which was able to conduct all fieldwork there. I am deeply indebted to the whole research team for this book project. I want to particularly thank Majed Abuazzam, Hala Abu Taleb, Jude Sajdi and Rawan Rbeihat. I am grateful to my research team in Cairo, without whom I would have had a very hard time conducting the research project. Even though Hatem Zayed was only present at the start of the project, his help in setting up the project was of immense importance. I want to thank Rana Gaber in particular for her hard work and dedication to the project. I am also thankful to Batoul Al-Mehdar, Alia Alaa Eddin, Bassant Bahaa El Din, Shaza Elewa, and Hood Ahmed for their work. This research team's enthusiasm, interest, and hard work throughout the project is a source of inspiration for me. I want to thank Pascale Ghazaleh, the HUSSLab and the Mellon Foundation for their generous support.

Many colleagues have read early drafts of different chapters, I am very grateful to their comments, which helped me further develop my argument. I want to particularly thank Dawn Brancati, Andrea Teti, Jillian Schwedler, Nathan Brown, Frederic Volpi, Eberhard Kienle, Federico Rossi and Lisa Anderson for their thoughtful reading and comments on different chapters. I am also very thankful to Irene Weipert-Fenner and Jonas Wolff for carefully reading some chapters and providing me with insightful comments. I am also grateful for them for hosting me as a guest scholar within their collaborative research project 'Contrust: Trust in Conflict-Political Life Under Conditions of Uncertainty' with Goethe University Frankfurt. During this time, I was able to complete writing the manuscript. I was also able to receive a lot of feedback from various scholars in both intuitions through the colloquium discussions and lecture. I am grateful to all colleagues in both institutions who took the time to read and comment on my work. I want to also thank the three peer reviewers of the manuscript for most helpful comments which helped me develop my argument and analysis.

I want to thank Dominic Byatt, the social science and humanities editor at Oxford University Press for his interest and consideration of the book project for publication. His help, support and efficiency during this whole endeavour has been of enormous help. I would like to thank Virginia Myers for editing the first draft of the book. I would also like to thank Hazel Haddon for editing the final draft.

Most importantly I would like to thank my family and friends for supporting me throughout this journey. I would have never completed this manuscript without their help, support and encouragement. My brother Adel made the last part of the writing process most intense, I have learned much from this experience. My son Tamer, my daughter Celine, my husband Edward, and my mother Mary, are my source of inspiration without whom my life would have been very boring.

Contents

Introduction: Civil Society and Activism in the Middle East: Regime Breakdown vs. Regime Continuity — 1
Civil Society in Authoritarian Regimes — 2
Civil Society and Social Movements — 3
Repressive Strategies in Authoritarian Regimes — 5
Case Selection and Research Method — 7
Outline of the Book — 9
Bibliography — 11

1. Civil Society, Activism, and Repression in Authoritarian Regimes — 16
Autocratization and Authoritarian Regime-Building — 16
Repression, Targets of Repression and Dissent — 19
Widespread versus Targeted Repression and Dissent — 22
Conceptualizing Civil Society — 25
The Agency of Civil Society in Authoritarian Regimes — 28
Authoritarian Regime-Building and Civil Society — 29
Authoritarian Regime Continuity and Civil Society — 30
The Consequences of International Support for Civil Society in Authoritarian Regimes — 33
Conclusion — 35
Bibliography — 36

2. Widespread Repression and Political Threats against Civil Society in Egypt — 44
Brief Historical Context from Nasser to Mubarak — 45
Dominating and Hegemonizing Civil Society — 47
Mubarak, Targeted Repression, and the Co-Optation of Civil Society — 48
The 25 January Uprising — 50
The Conflict–Dissent Nexus — 50
From the Fall of Mubarak to the Fall of Morsi: A New Beginning in Widespread Repression — 51
The 30 June 'Revolution' — 54
Repression and Fear as Tools against Mobilization and Dissent — 56
Controlling CSOs through GONGOs — 62
Building Government–Civil Society Partnerships — 64
Political Opportunities and Repression — 65
Conclusion — 67
Bibliography — 68

3. Activism and Demobilization in Egypt — 72
- The Conflict–Dissent Nexus — 73
- The Raba'a Square Massacre — 74
- Islamist Movements — 77
- The Muslim Brotherhood and Repression — 79
- The Institutionalization of Repression — 80
- Repression and Demobilization — 80
- The Tiran and Sanafir Controversy — 84
- Conclusion — 87
- Bibliography — 87

4. Political Context, Co-Optation, and Targeted Repression in Jordan — 91
- The Repression–Concession Nexus — 92
- Black September and Its Consequences — 93
- Balancing Targeted Repression and Concession after Black September — 94
- A New Wave of Contentious Events — 95
- The Co-Optation of Political Parties — 97
- The Impact of Concessions on Participation — 99
- The Uprisings of 2011 and the Changing Political Context — 101
- Concessions after the Arab Uprisings — 102
- The Fourth Circle Demonstrations — 105
- Field Opportunity Structures and Targeted Repression — 107
- Targeted Repression and Its Discontents: Internal Splits — 109
- Conclusion — 113
- Bibliography — 114

5. Coalition Partnerships in Light of Concessions and Targeted Repression in Jordan — 118
- Economic Reforms for Social Control — 119
- Concessions to Civil Society as a Form of Control — 121
- Women's Organizations and Activism after the Arab Uprisings — 123
- Coalition-Building and Networks — 125
- The Impact of Concessions and Targeted Repression on Women's Rights Coalitions — 126
- The Concession–Repression Nexus — 130
- Linkages between Field and Political Opportunity Structures — 132
- Islamists in Civil Society — 133
- International Support for Civil Society and Regime Legitimation — 135
- Conclusion — 137
- Bibliography — 138

Conclusion **143**
Different Types of Repression in Response to Dissent 144
Reassessing the Repression–Dissent and the Concession–
  Repression Nexus 146
The Consequences of Different Modes of Repression on Civil Society 147
From Breakdown to Repression and Back Again? 149
Bibliography 150

Index 153

Introduction
Civil Society and Activism in the Middle East

Regime Breakdown vs. Regime Continuity

Why do authoritarian regimes utilize different repressive strategies towards civil society actors? How do these actors respond to these strategies to mobilize and advance social, economic, and political change? In this book I argue that authoritarian regimes' repressive strategies towards civil society actors vary depending on each regime's recent historical experience with regime breakdown and/or continuity. Authoritarian regimes that go through breakdown and that transition from one autocratic rule to another increase repression against all civil society actors while targeting the political opposition in an effort to pre-empt large-scale mobilization. This instils fear into civil society actors, who as a result either disengage from civic and political activism or turn to different forms of participation, such as social entrepreneurship. On the other hand, long-standing authoritarian regimes that have not faced breakdown utilize targeted repression and co-optation strategies while tolerating civic and political activism, as well as some forms of contentious activities. Civil society actors in these regimes are able to grasp political opportunities to mobilize for demonstrations at certain times and in certain spaces, and to develop coalition partnerships to push the regime to advance some reforms and change.

I test this argument through an in-depth analysis of two case studies in the Middle East, Egypt and Jordan. These two cases shed light on different mechanisms and processes within authoritarian regimes and show how a regime's perception of public mobilization and civil society is shaped by that regime's own recent historical experience with authoritarian breakdown or continuity. They also demonstrate the consequences of different types of repression on civil society actors and mobilization processes in authoritarian regimes. In doing so, the book adds to the burgeoning literature on the consequences of targeted and widespread repression in authoritarian regimes, providing a nuanced analysis of the different types of repressive strategies employed in authoritarian regimes within the same region. It also adds to the literature on social movements through analysing how different types of repressive strategies, mainly targeted and widespread repression, impact civil society actors and their capacity to mobilize, build coalition partnerships and networks, and advance change in their polities. It further demonstrates how different types of repressive strategies can demobilize large-scale and small-scale protests in the short and long run.

Civil Society in Authoritarian Regimes

Scholarly debates on civil society in authoritarian regimes are abundant. Most research analyses civil society either as contributing to democratization (Norton 1995; O'Donnell et al. 1986; Diamond 1999; Teorell 2010), or as a tool for authoritarian resilience (Yom 2005; Cavatorta and Durac 2010; Kienle 2007). The literature analysing how civil society contributes to authoritarian resilience contends that authoritarian regimes have a dual strategy towards civil society. On the one hand, they use specific laws to co-opt and restrict civil society actors who work in charitable, socioeconomic, and cultural development organizations. On the other hand, they repress civil society actors whom they consider to be in political opposition, such as protest movements or human rights activists. In Russia, for instance, those civil society actors who are politically active in opposition movements are repressed, while the regime co-opts other civil society actors whose main function is to work for socioeconomic development and to mobilize society in favour of the regime (Cheskin and March 2015). It is largely assumed that all authoritarian regimes use these strategies towards civil society actors, without differentiating between authoritarian regime types or authoritarian regimes' recent experiences with breakdown and/or continuity. Thus it is believed that the strategies of today's authoritarian regimes towards civil society are similar to those of Russia—tolerating some actors and repressing others (Sika 2022).[1] Nevertheless, looking at the Middle East in the aftermath of the 2011 Arab uprisings, we see that authoritarian regimes in the region use different strategies towards civil society actors. In Egypt, for instance, the regime has intensified its repression towards all civil society actors since 2013. In Jordan, however, the regime uses targeted repression only against opposition actors, while tolerating and co-opting the rest.

---

[1] This assumption has mainly been made by post-democratization scholars whose work reflects cases in the aftermath of the third wave of democracy.

Previous research on targeted and widespread repression contends that authoritarian regimes that are concerned about public contention and mobilization use less violence against their citizens. According to Greitens (2016, 12), for instance, authoritarian regimes are normally in favour of 'limiting violence rather than increasing it'. The empirical evidence presented in this book, however, shows that this is not necessarily the case for all authoritarian regimes. The type of repression used is dependent on various factors, like the regime's perception of threat from public mobilization, the regime's recent experiences with large-scale mobilization, and whether these mobilization and contentious events have had an impact on regime breakdown or not. I show here that authoritarian regimes which have experienced regime breakdown as a result of public mobilization, and which are undergoing an autocratization process, utilize both widespread and targeted repression. They utilize widespread repression against all civil society actors, while also targeting political opposition. On the other hand, authoritarian regimes that have been resilient in response to public mobilization use less violence and targeted repression.

The inquiry in this book is twofold: first, I analyse why and how authoritarian regimes utilize different strategies towards civil society actors in light of the literature on authoritarianism and autocratization. I augment the literature on comparative authoritarianism by analysing state strategies towards civil society actors. Here, I differentiate between the strategies of long-lasting autocratic regimes and those of regimes that experienced a breakdown and are undergoing an autocratization and authoritarian regime-building process. I demonstrate how the strategies of each regime type towards civil society differ. Second, I employ social movement literature, mainly the mechanism and processes approach (McAdam et al. 2001) to examine civil society actors, how they react to their political context, and how they interact with the prevalent political opportunities and threats when exposed to different repressive strategies.

Civil Society and Social Movements

Research on civil society mostly disregards the literature and research tools from social movement studies (Rossi and Della Porta 2009; Della Porta 2020), even though both civil society and social movements utilize the political context, with its opportunities and threats, to advance change in their respective polities. This book relies on Diani's (2015) relational mode of collective action's modes of coordination, and the categorization of social movements as a different type of social networks. When we analyse the modes of coordination among actors and networks, we will be able to understand the 'distinctiveness of social movements as a particular form of collective action, while locating them firmly within the broader civil society dynamics' (Diani 2015, 5). Civil society is not confined to formal organizations, but also includes various networks, social movement actors, activists, unions, non-governmental organizations (NGO)s, syndicates, coalition partners, and campaigns. It contains religious organizations and political parties, because they move from the political to the civic spheres (Härdig 2015; Stolleis 2018; Al-Sayyid 1995; Della Porta 2020). In such instances, social movements can belong to civil society, since they consist of actors who are not institutionalized and who belong to different groups, and whose activities trigger social and political conflicts. These actors in and of themselves work to change institutional settings and cultural interactions in various ways (Della Porta 2020; Alexander 2006). In return, civil society reacts to the opportunities and threats of the political context by utilizing different framing techniques and repertoires of contention. When there is a closing of the public sphere and civil society actors perceive a political threat, they move to entrepreneurship, independent and informal activities. On the other hand, when political opportunity is more open and accessible, they resort to coalition-building, networking, and protest activities to advance change.

The political context, with its opportunities and threats, is a framework for understanding how these factors have given rise to liberalization measures that have in turn shaped and influenced civil society actors and their impact in the polity. This approach allows us to see how these various processes have impacted civil society actors and how these actors have impacted their polity. Hence, we have a better understanding of how and why coalition-building, networking, and the eruption of protest events occur at certain times and in certain spaces and not others. We also understand why demobilization occurs at particular times, while mobilization occurs at others. Without understanding the political context, we cannot address and understand activists' ability to impact politics from below (Kitchelt 1986; Kriesi 2004; MacAdam et al. 2008; Tarrow and Tilly 2006; Tilly et al. 2001; Ancelovici 2021). Building on this approach, I follow Volpi and Clark's (2019) interactionist orientation, which analyses both the contextual macro level and the micro level, but I also look at the agency of civil society actors, and of other social and political players, who influence and are influenced by the structure of the opportunities and threats under which they live. These interactions demonstrate what is achieved by civil society actors and how and when mobilization or demobilization occur.

Repressive Strategies in Authoritarian Regimes

Repression refers to 'the actual or threatened use of physical sanctions against an individual or organization, within the territorial jurisdiction of the state, for the purpose of imposing a cost on the target as well as deterring specific activities and/or beliefs perceived to be challenging to government personnel, practices or intuitions' (Goldstein 1978, xxvii in Davenport 2007, 2).[2] Repression also encompasses different coercive efforts that are used by the regime to influence individuals within their territories. These include 'overt and covert; violent and nonviolent; state, state-sponsored (e.g., militias), and state-affiliated (e.g., death squads); successful and unsuccessful' (Davenport 2007, 3).

Most research on repression and mobilization generally treats all types of repressive strategies as one unit and does not distinguish between different strategies of repression. Rather, it analyses its function and impact on mobilization and demobilization (Nugent 2020; Davenport 2007). According to Josua and Edel (2015), forms of repression are distinctive based on whether they are 'contained' or 'incapacitating'. Contained repression is primarily the checks that a regime faces on certain types of repressive actions. Incapacitating repression on the other hand, is deployed when a regime faces a crisis, mostly through mass mobilization, and hence deploys large-scale repression. Different modes of repression thus influence participation and mobilization differently and hence, repression does not influence different contexts similarly (Bourdreau 2009).

Since different modes of repression impact participation differently, a closer look at targeted and widespread repression can illuminate the consequences of different forms of repression on civic and political participation and mobilization. Targeted repression is when a regime identifies certain individuals and/or organizations as politically threatening and hence chooses to eliminate them through arrest, disappearance, or killing (Gohdes 2020). This type of repression is believed to be the most frequently used strategy of repression in authoritarian regimes. Yet it is also believed to be the most preferred type of repression in autocracies (Xu 2021; Sullivan 2016; Greitens 2016). Moreover, some scholars argue that when repression is targeted at certain groups but not others, it is more effective at demobilization, since it is capable of dividing the opposition against one another (Nugent 2020). This

---

[2] This section relies heavily on Nadine Sika. 2023. 'Mobilization, repression and policy concessions in authoritarian regimes: The cases of Egypt and Jordan'. *Political Studies.* https://doi.org/10.1177/00323217221141426

strategy is important as a tool for pre-empting and eliminating all types of opposition activism against a certain regime (Demirel-Pegg and Rasler 2017).

Scholars concerned with analysing the consequences of widespread repression argue that it has a more negative effect on the authoritarian regime than on civil society actors. For instance, it can cause the international community to impose sanctions on the regime, or it can increase public mobilization against the regime (Xu 2021; Davenport 2007; Sullivan 2016). Widespread mobilization can thus lead to a 'backfire outcome' (Demirel-Pegg and Rasler 2021) in which the opposition can increase their mobilizational capacities in response to increased repression. Recently, scholars have argued that personalist regimes are more likely to utilize widespread repression, since they do not have the institutional capacity to co-opt their opposition like dominant party regimes, for instance. Nevertheless, the case of Egypt which will be further analysed in the coming chapters proves otherwise, since widespread repression against all forms of civil society actors has been the norm rather than the exception since 2013. Since this date until the writing of this book, no large-scale mass mobilization has taken place, and civil society has been fragmented and weakened.

I build on these debates by incorporating these distinctions within the conflict–repression nexus (Davenport and Moore 2012; Lichbach 1987; deMeritt 2016; al-Anani 2019; Davenport et al. 2022), which will be analysed in the chapters on Egypt to understand the extent to which widespread repression against civil society actors influences public participation and mobilization processes. The main concern of this strand of research is to understand the extent to which repression leads to demobilization. Here the 'Law of Coercive Response' (Davenport 2007, 7), which purports that regimes respond to increasing threats with more violence, is helpful. When a regime instils fear in citizens and activists alike, it can stop them from participating in mobilization or dissent. Instilling fear in this regard is an important repertoire for the regime, because it makes individuals less likely to risk becoming part of collective action. Most important is how regimes perceive this threat. In regimes where breakdown, autocratization, and authoritarian regime-building processes are taking place, the perception of threat can come from any civil society actor, be it charity organization, developmental organization, or human rights organization, that could potentially have the ability to mobilize.

The alternative concession–repression nexus (Rasler 1996; Franklin 2015; Sika 2019; Young 2021; Ma and Cheng 2020) is analysed in the chapters on Jordan, where the regime utilizes targeted repression towards the political opposition and some movements, while utilizing concessions during major contentious events, as will be shown in Chapters 4 and 5. Widespread repression from this perspective is costly, and authoritarian regimes may therefore decide to use some other techniques to fend off public mobilization. Providing material and political concessions, like access to affordable healthcare and more political liberalization processes, are different forms of concessions. These strategies develop into political opportunities for mobilization and contestation while at the same time helping to prevent mass demonstrations from occurring.

Case Selection and Research Method

The Middle East and North Africa (MENA) has long been analysed within the post-democratization literature as a region where the coercive apparatus plays an instrumental part in authoritarian resilience (Bellin 2004; Nugent 2020; Josua and Edel 2021).[3] Since the advent of the Arab uprisings in 2010–2011, the importance of a 'shared identity, history, and culture' have been essential in how demonstrations and mobilization processes diffused from one country to the other in the region (Bellin 2012). These shared identities and process of mobilization are important for the general comparative analysis with other authoritarian regimes. Previous studies on comparative politics have advocated for the importance of intra-regional comparisons (Basedau and Köllner 2007; Bank 2018). This comparative analysis can be advantageous where some background conditions like history, culture, socioeconomic standards, and political institutions and structures are similar (Bank 2018). Since the Arab uprisings, the level and scope of repression has been increasing (Josua and Edel 2021). Given the pervasive use of coercion in this region, analysing why various forms of repression are utilized at certain times and in certain spaces will add to the general understanding of the consequences of repression in authoritarian regimes. I build on the differences between the regime types of republics and monarchies in the region, especially since Egypt is an authoritarian republic and Jordan an absolutist monarchy. Yet I also go beyond the institutional analysis of monarchical exceptionalism in MENA to understand how and why two authoritarian regimes in one region utilize different strategies of repression, and what the consequences of these different repressive strategies are for civil society actors.

---

[3] In this section I build on previous work I have carried out on the case studies of Jordan and Egypt in the research method and case selection in Nadine Sika. 2023. 'Mobilization, repression and policy concessions in authoritarian regimes: The cases of Egypt and Jordan'. *Political Studies*. https://doi.org/10.1177/00323217221141426

To advance a nuanced understanding of this process, I employ comparative historical analysis (CHA). In this approach, mechanisms are studied through observing them at the individual level via empirical evidence. Demonstrating that hypothesized causes can covary in different cases is not sufficient in CHA. 'Rather, the researcher must provide the reasons why this is so by opening up the black box and identifying the steps that connect observed causes to observed outcomes' (Thelen and Mahoney 2015, 15). Much like research based on case studies, the analysis here is based on the mechanisms that are empirically identified. Hence, the main task in CHA is to identify the processes that are linked together through a nuanced analysis to demonstrate that the main set of casual factors that were hypothesized by the researcher influence the outcome. 'This kind of empirically grounded mechanism-based explanation requires delving into the details and thus demands a deep understanding of the cases under analysis' (Thelen and Mahoney 2015, 16). This analysis also contributes to our understanding of why regimes that have similar institutional backgrounds differ in their resilience regarding autocracy and why authoritarian regimes respond differently to similar exogenous or endogenous social/economic 'shocks'.

This approach is helpful for the analysis of Egypt and Jordan, since the two cases will each be thoroughly analysed to understand three interrelated mechanisms. First, the research identifies the impact of authoritarian regime breakdown, autocratization, and authoritarian regime-building in the case of Egypt, versus authoritarian regime continuity in the case of Jordan. This impacts these regimes' own perception of threat from civil society in general and from public mobilization in particular. Then the ensuing strategies of widespread versus targeted repression towards civil society actors by each regime will be examined, to further understand how perceptions of threat are related to the types of repressive strategies utilized towards civil society actors. Finally, the consequences of these various forms of repression on civil society activism, mobilization, coalition- and network-building processes, in addition to demobilization, will be investigated. This detailed analysis can be achieved through process tracing, which focuses on the development and unfolding of different events over specified periods of time.

> Yet grasping this unfolding is impossible if one cannot adequately describe an event or situation *at one point in time*. Hence, the *descriptive* component of process tracing begins not with observing change or sequence, but rather with taking good snapshots at a series of specific moments. To characterize a process, we must be

able to characterize key steps in the process, which in turn permits good analysis of change and sequence.

(Collier 2021, 824)

This approach also helps the researcher to develop comparative analysis across cases (Bennett and Checkel 2015; Nugent 2020). Hence, when we analyse an authoritarian regime's strategies towards civil society actors and how these actors react through understanding their own encounters and narratives of events, we can see a comparative analysis across cases. These are described in semi-structured interviews and focus groups, where we are able to understand how different repressive strategies contribute to different forms of civil society activism.

The analysis is dependent on qualitative analysis through process tracing, semi-structured interviews, and focus groups with more than 150 civil society actors in Egypt and Jordan. In Egypt, 116 semi-structured interviews and three focus groups were conducted with civil society actors, and in Jordan, fifty-two semi-structured interviews were carried out. Fieldwork for the interviews and focus groups was conducted between May and November 2018. In Egypt, all except five interviews were held in Cairo. In Jordan, the majority of interviews were conducted in Amman, but the research team also reached out to civil society actors in Irbid, Karak, Tafileh, Al Salt, and Jarash. The selection process of these actors was based on mapping different NGOs, protest movement actors, human rights organizations, and unions in each country. From these we selected a convenience sample through targeting different members of civil society organizations to conduct interviews. After the first round of interviews, the research was based on snowball sampling—in each interview we asked interviewees to suggest other interview subjects (Sika 2019; Salganik and Heckathorn 2004). Although this method has a few problems, especially when making generalizations or inferences, and also carries some selection bias, it is still useful for the purposes of this study (Creswell and Guetterman 2019). When the public sphere is constrained under an authoritarian context and activists are hard to reach, we can rely on this method not to advance generalizations, but to develop an in-depth analysis of the political context.

Outline of the Book

This book consists of five chapters, as well as an 'Introduction' and a 'Conclusion'. In the 'Introduction', the main argument and research methods of the book are developed. Chapter 1 answers the question of why varying historical experiences influence authoritarian regimes differently and how they impact these regimes' repressive strategies towards civil society actors. Why do some authoritarian regimes resort to widespread repression against civil society actors, while others resort to targeted repression? In this chapter I analyse these questions by shedding light on major debates concerning different modes of repression in authoritarian regimes and through conceptualizing civil society. I argue that an autocratization process after regime breakdown is like a state-building process and is characterized by an increase in the use of coercion and repression against social actors. Thus regimes which have foreseen breakdown and are in the process of authoritarian regime-building increase their repressive strategies towards civil society. They want to build their reputation for ferocity, but at the same time they want to build consent through hegemonizing the public sphere. On the other hand, in resilient authoritarian regimes that do not face imminent threats to their existence, co-optation of the majority of civil society actors is rather the norm, while repression is the exception. I then go on to demonstrate that civil society is both a contested and a cooperative space in which the regime and social actors either cooperate or contest each other's legitimacy, depending on the time and space in which an authoritarian regime is situated.

Chapter 2 examines the case of Egypt and answers the question: why did the regime increase its repressive strategies against all civil society actors in the aftermath of the 25 January uprising? How did the political context develop political threats constraining civil society's ability to build coalition partnerships and networks, or to mobilize for certain campaigns advocating for socioeconomic or political change? In this chapter I argue that, in their attempt to demobilize the public, regimes undergoing autocratization processes after breakdown like Egypt deem it necessary to utilize widespread repressive measures to demobilize the public and to avert any attempt at mobilization, even small-scale mobilization. In this chapter I analyse the political context, which not only addresses the environment or the causes of different sociopolitical phenomena, but also demonstrates the impact of different factors on the outcome of certain phenomena in the polity, while not directly causing them.

In Chapter 3, I zoom in on the Egyptian regime's repressive strategies against 'politicized' civil society actors, namely human rights organizations, independent activists, student unions, political parties, and movements. I engage with debates pertaining to the conflict–dissent nexus. I demonstrate that in the short run, a regime undergoing an authoritarian regime-building process increases its repressive measures, which in turn have the effect of demobilizing the public. When a political opportunity is prevalent for mobilization, activists utilize it to their advantage; however, mobilizations under extreme repression become fewer in number and shorter in duration.

In Chapter 4 I analyse the case of Jordan, examining the political and historical contexts with their political opportunities and threats as a means to understand how these have led to political liberalization measures, which in turn have shaped and influenced the presence of civil society and its ability to mobilize for change. To what extent has the Jordanian regime utilized repression towards political activists? How do activists respond and mobilize in turn? This chapter demonstrates how the regime relies on an amalgam of targeted repression and concessions. It further demonstrates how civil society is capable of utilizing the political opportunities and threats to their own advantage to mobilize for different campaigns that are concerned with advancing socioeconomic and political change.

In Chapter 5 I analyse the political context, which is not merely an environment or a direct cause of certain sociopolitical phenomena. For the analysis in this chapter, I add both the social field and the political field. Jordan is interesting in this regard because different social actors target different institutions. For instance, we see women's NGOs, which constitute the women's movement, target social traditions, private sector firms, and the regime. Hence, it is not only the regime that is of concern to these movements, but other social institutions at large. Unlike in Egypt, the Jordanian regime does not attempt to demobilize the public through constraining civil society actors who work in the developmental field.

In the conclusion, I compare and contrast the different regime strategies and repertoires of repression and concession towards civil society actors in Egypt and Jordan. I further discuss the mobilization and demobilization strategies of civil society actors in both countries. I draw some conclusions on the region and suggest further research directions for contentious politics in authoritarian regimes.

Bibliography

Alexander, Jeffery. 2006. *The Civil Sphere*. Oxford: Oxford University Press.
Al-Sayyid, Mustapha. 1995. 'The concept of civil society and the Arab world'. In *Political Liberalization and Democratization in the Arab World*, Vol. 1, by Rex Brynen, Bahgat Korany, and Paul Noble, 131–147. Boulder: Lynne Rienner.

al-Anani, Khalil. 2019. 'Rethinking the repression-dissent nexus: Assessing Egypt's Muslim Brotherhood's response to repression since the coup of 2013'. *Democratization* 26 (8): 1329–1341.

Ancelovici, Marcos. 2021. 'Conceptualizing the context of collective action: An introduction'. *Social Movement Studies* 20 (2): 125–138.

Bank, André. 2018. 'Comparative area studies in the study of Middle East politics after the Arab uprisings'. In *Comparative Area Studies: Methodological Rationales and Cross-Regional Applications*, by Ariel Ahram, Patrick Köllner, and Rudra Sil, 119–132. Oxford: Oxford University Press.

Basedau, Matthias and Patrick Köllner. 2007. 'Area studies, comparative area studies, and the study of politics: Context, substance, and methodological challenges'. *Zeitschrift für Vergleichende Politische Wissenschaft* 1 (1): 105–124. https://doi.org/10.1007/s12286-007-0009-3

Bellin, Eva. 2004. 'The robustness of authoritarianism in the Middle East: Exceptionalism in comparative perspective'. *Comparative Politics* 36 (2): 139–157.

Bellin, Eva. 2012. 'Reconsidering authoritarianism in the Arab World'. *Comparative Politics* 44 (2): 127–149.

Bennett, Andrew and Jeffrey Checkel. 2015. *Process Tracing: From Metaphor to Analytic Tool*. Cambridge, UK: Cambridge University Press.

Boudreau, Vince. 2009. *Resisting Dictatorship: Repression and Protest in Southeast Asia*. Cambridge: Cambridge University Press.

Cavatorta, Francesco and Vincent Durac. 2010. *Civil Society and Democratization in the Arab World: The Dynamics of Activism*. London: Routledge.

Cheskin, Ammon and Luke March. 2015. 'State–society relations in contemporary Russia: New forms of political and social contention'. *East European Politics* 31 (3): 261–273.

Collier, David. 2021. 'Understanding process tracing'. *PS: Political Science and Politics* 44 (4): 823–830.

Conrad, Courtenay. 2011. 'Constrained concessions: Beneficent dictatorial responses to the domestic political opposition'. *International Studies Quarterly* 55: 1167–1187.

Creswell, John, and Timothy Guetterman. 2019. *Educational Research: Planning, Conducting, an Evaluating Quantitative and Qualitative Research 6th Edition*. Indianapolis: Merrill Education.

Davenport, Christian. 2007. 'State repression and political order'. *Annual Review of Political Science* 10: 1–23.

Davenport, Christian and Hill Moore. 2012. 'The Arab Spring, winter, and back again? (Re)Introducing the dissent-repression nexus with a twist'. *International Interactions: Empirical and Theoretical Research in International Relations* 38 (5): 704–713.

Davenport, Christian, Babak RazaeeDaryakenari, and Reem Wood. 2022. 'Tenure through tyranny? Repression, dissent, and leader removal in Africa and Latin America, 1990–2006'. *Journal of Global Security Studies* 7 (1): 1–17.

Della Porta, Donatella. 2020. 'Building bridges: Social movements and civil society in times of crisis'. *Voluntas* 31: 938–948.

deMeritt, Jacqueline H. R. 2016. 'The strategic use of state repression and political violence'. *Oxford Research Encyclopedia of Politics* DOI: 10.1093/acrefore/9780190228637.013.32.

Demirel-Pegg, Tijen and Karen Rasler. 2017. 'Protesters Under the Gun: Under What Conditions do States Manage Backfire Effects Successfully'. *Annual Meeting of the International Studies Association.*

Demirel-Pegg, Tijen and Karen Rasler. 2021. 'The effects of selective and indiscriminate repression on the 2013 Gezi park nonviolent resistance campaign'. *Sociological Perspectives*, 64 (1): 58–81. https://doi.org/10.1177/0731121420914291

Diamond, Larry. 1999. *Developing Democracy: Toward Consolidation*. Baltimore: Johns Hopkins University Press.

Diani, Mario. 2015. *The Cement of Civil Society: Studying Networks in Localities.* Cambridge: Cambridge University Press.

Doug McAdam, Sidney Tarrow, and Chalres Tilly. 2001. *Dynamics of Contention.* Cambridge: Cambridge University Press.

Franklin, James. 2015. 'Persistent challengers: Repression, concessions, challenger strength, and commitment in Latin America'. *Mobilization: An International Quarterly* 20 (1): 61–80.

Franz, Erica, Andrea Kendall-Taylor, Joseph Wright, and Xu Xu. 2020. 'Personalization of power and repression in dictatorships'. *Journal of Politics* 82 (1): 372–377.

Gohdes, Anita. 2020. 'Repression technology: Internet accessibility and state violence'. *American Journal of Political Science* 64 (3): 488–503.

Goldstein, Robert Justin. 1978. *Political Repression in Modern America: From 1870 to the Present*. Cambridge, MA: Schenkman.

Greitens, Sheena Chestnut. 2016. *Dictators and their Secret Police: Coercive Institutions and State Violence*. Cambridge, MA: Cambridge University Press.

Hager, Anselm and Krzystof Krakowski. 2022. 'Does state repression spark protests? Evidence from secret police surveillance in communist Poland'. *American Political Science Review* 116 (2): 564–579.

Härdig, Anders. 2015. 'Beyond the Arab revolts: Conceptualizing civil society in the Middle East and North Africa'. *Democratization* 22 (6): 1131–1153.

Josua, Maria and Mirjam Edel. 2015. 'To repress or not to repress-regime survival strategies in the Arab Spring'. *Terrorism and Political Violence* 27 (2): 289–309.

Josua, Maria and Mirjam Edel. 2021. 'The Arab uprisings and the return of repression'. *Mediterranean Politics* 26 (5): 586–611.

Kienle, Eberhard. 2007. *Democracy Promotion and the Renewal of Authoritarian Rule*. By Oliver Schlumberger. Stanford: Stanford University Press, 231–250.

Kitchelt, Herbert. 1986. 'Political opportunity structures and political protest: Anti-Nuclear movements in four democracies'. *British Journal of Political Science* 16 (1): 57–85.

Kriesi, Hanspeter. 2004. 'Political context and opportunity'. In *The Blackwell Companion to Social Movements*, by David Snow, Sarah Soule, and Hanspeter Kriesi. Malden: Blackwell Publishing, 67–90.

Levitsky, Steven and Lucan Way. 2015. 'Not just what, but when (and how): comparative-historical approaches to authoritarian durability'. In *Advances in Comparative-Historical Analysis*, by James Mahoney and Kathleen Thelen. Cambridge: Cambridge University Press, 97–120.

Lichbach, Mark Irving. 1987. 'Deterrence or escalation?: The puzzle of aggregate studies of repression and dissent'. *Journal of Conflict Resolution* 31 (2): 266–297.

Ma, Ngok and Edmund W. Cheng. 2020. *The Umbrella Movement: Civil Resistance and Contentious Space in Hong Kong*, Revised Edn. Amsterdam: Amsterdam University Press.

Norton, Augustus Richard. 1995. *Civil Society in the Middle East*. Leiden: E. J. Brill.

Nugent, Elizabeth. 2020. *After Repression: How Polarization Derails Democratic Transition*. Princeton: Princeton University Press.

O'Donnell, Guillermo, Philippe Schmitter, and Laurence Whitehead. 1986. *Transitions from Authoritarian Rule*. Baltimore: Johns Hopkins University Press.

Rasler, Karen. 1996. 'Concessions, repression, and political protest in the Iranian revolution'. *American Sociological Review* 61 (1): 132–152.

Rossi, Federico and Donatella della Porta. 2009. 'Social movement, trade unions and advocacy networks'. In *Democratization*, by Christian Haerpfer, Patrick Berbhagen, Ronald Inglehart, and Christian Welzel, 172–185. Oxford: Oxford University Press.

Salganik, Mathew, and Douglas Heckathorn. 2004. 'Sampling and estimation in hidden populations using respondent-driven sampling'. *Sociological Methodology* 34 (1): 193–239.

Seawright, Jason and John Gerring. 2008. 'Case selection techniques in case study research: A menu of qualitative and quantitative options'. *Political Research Quarterly* 61 (2): 294–308.

Sika, Nadine. 2019. 'Repression, cooptation and movement fragmentation: Evidence from the youth movement in Egypt'. *Political Studies* 67 (3): 676–692.

Stolleis, Friederike. 2018. 'Civic engagement'. In *Coping with Uncertainty: Youth in the Middle East and North Africa*, by Jörg Gertel and Ralph Hexel. London: Saqi, 279–297.

Sullivan, Christopher M. 2016. 'Political repression and the destruction of dissident organizations: Evidence from the archives of the Guatemalan National Police'. *World Politics* 68 (4):645–676.

Tarrow, Sidney. 1998. *Power in Movement: Social Movements and Contentious Politics*. New York: Cambridge University Press.

Teorell, Jean. 2010. *Determinants of Democratization: Explaining Regime Change in the World, 1972–2006*. Cambridge: Cambridge University Press. 2-10.

Thelen, Kathrleen and James Mahoney. 2015. 'Comparative-historical analysis in contemporary political science'. In *Advances in Comparative-Historical Analysis*, by James Mahoney and Kathleen Thelen. Cambridge: Cambridge University Press, 3–36.

Tilly, Charles and Sidney Tarrow. 2006. *Contentious Politics*. Oxford: Oxford University Press.

Volpi, Frédéric and Janine Clark. 2019. 'Activism in the Middle East and North Africa in times of upheaval: Social networks' actions and interactions'. *Social Movement Studies* 18 (1): 1–16.

Xu, Xu. 2021. 'To repress or to co-opt? Authoritarian control in the Age of Digital Surveillance'. *American Journal of Political Science* 65 (2): 309–325.

Yom, Sean. 2005. 'Civil society and democratization in the Arab world'. *Middle East Review of International Affairs* 9 (4): 14–33.

Young, Sokphea. 2021. *Civil Society Organisations versus the Ruler: A Zero-Sum Game?* Singapore: Palgrave Macmillan.

1
Civil Society, Activism, and Repression in Authoritarian Regimes

Why do different authoritarian regime types utilize different repressive strategies towards civil society actors? In this chapter I approach this question by examining the major debates about post-democratization theory and the burgeoning literature on autocratization, in addition to conceptualizing civil society. I demonstrate that an authoritarian regime-building process, like a state-building process, is characterized by an increased use of violence and repression against social actors. Thus, regimes that have foreseen breakdown and are in the process of authoritarian regime-building escalate their repressive strategies towards civil society through utilizing widespread repression. They want to heighten their reputation for ferocity, but at the same time to build consent through hegemonizing the public sphere. In resilient authoritarian regimes, where regime breakdown has not occurred and there is no imminent threat to the regime's existence, co-optation of the majority of civil society actors in addition to targeted repression of opposition actors is rather the norm. Civil society is both a contested and a cooperative space, where a regime and societal actors either cooperate with or contest each other's legitimacy, depending on the time and space in which the authoritarian regime is situated.

Autocratization and Authoritarian Regime-Building

The burgeoning literature on autocratization purports that autocratization is 'a matter of degree that can occur both in democracies and autocracies'. It also denotes 'any move away from [full] democracy' (Lührmann and Lindberg 2019, 1099). When analysing democratic traits, scholars assume the presence of some procedural democratic institutions like elections or parliaments which are also present in autocracies. Hence, an autocratization process occurring in authoritarian regimes can take place in authoritarian regimes whereby democratic institutions become less effective and more

Civil Society and Activism in the Middle East. Nadine Sika, Oxford University Press. © Nadine Sika (2024).
DOI: 10.1093/oso/9780198882411.003.0002

authoritarian traits are exhibited. Most autocracies exhibit some democratic regime traits in varying degrees. For instance, they might have competitive elections that are not free and fair, which can erode with time to become non-competitive elections (Lührmann and Lindberg 2019).

Autocratization includes both sudden '"breakdowns of democracy" *á la* Linz and gradual processes within and outside of democratic regimes where democratic traits decline—resulting in less democratic, or more autocratic situations' (Lührmann and Lindberg 2019, 1099). This strand of research distinguishes itself from the democratization literature through demonstrating that autocratization does not necessarily happen after democratic breakdown, but can actually occur after a regime has already been democratic for a while, as in the case of Hungary, for instance (Lührmann and Lindberg 2019). Moreover, it is not easy to gauge the start of the autocratization process, since most of the time it happens gradually. Thus autocratization can consist of three different modes: 1) democratic backsliding or recession; 2) democratic breakdown, or the collapse of a democratic regime; and 3) authoritarian consolidation, whereby democratic institutions and qualities are eroded in democracies and/or autocracies alike (Pelke and Croissant 2021). Autocratization and democratic backsliding have been occurring worldwide throughout the past decade (Hellmeier et al. 2020).

This line of research is distinct from the democratization or the transitology paradigm, since its assumption is that the starting point of autocratization can either be 'democratic breakdown,' the gradual erosion of democratic institutions and/or an authoritarian regime that is deepening authoritarian institutions and instantaneously diminishing democratic institutions. Democratization and transitology, on the other hand, assume that a democratic transition occurs after an authoritarian regime breakdown. My assumption here bridges the distinction of these two strands of literature and shows that autocratization also occurs after authoritarian regime breakdown. I also look at civil society from below to understand how regime breakdown and the ensuing authoritarian regime building process and autocratization impact civil society actors. This provides 'a broadening of the focus to the society level through the integration of insights from the recent debate on social (non-) movements and from parts of the classic democratization literature' (Valbjørn 2014, 159).

I then demonstrate that there is a distinction in the repressive authoritarian strategies employed by regimes that have undergone breakdown compared to those that are deepening their authoritarian traits. Here, one case study, that of Egypt, analyses authoritarian regime breakdown where an autocratization process ensues. The other case study, that of Jordan, analyses authoritarian endurance followed by an autocratization process. Taking this into consideration, I follow the transitology assumptions in the case of Egypt, which start *after* authoritarian regime breakdown. However, instead of analysing the 'democratization' process after breakdown, I look at the autocratization process. Thus, as in transitology, the main assumption is that the first few years after breakdown are most violent and unstable. Here, a situation of 'rapid and unpredictable change, high risk, shifting interests and indeterminate strategic reactions' occurs (Schmitter 2014, 73). Thus, in an autocratizing regime undergoing authoritarian regime-building, autocratization entails the use of widespread violence to control the polity. Authoritarian breakdown, authoritarian regime-building and autocratization, like state-building, are accompanied by violence, since a newly emerging regime, like a newly established state, wants to eradicate its internal rivals so as to extract more resources from the polity (Tilly 1993; Skocpol 1994). Regime-building, like state-building, is 'a violent process because it threatens the interests of recalcitrant actors and it encounters outlying resistance which must be suppressed' (Newman 2013, 141). Populism is utilized extensively in such cases to justify coercion against civil society actors and all political opposition (Trantidis 2021). Similarly, when analysing post-revolutionary regimes which are 'transitioning' from one regime to another, Lachapelle and his colleagues (2020) argue that one of the major reasons for the endurance of authoritarian revolutionary regimes is their excessive reliance on widespread repression and coercion, and these regimes' ability to destroy any alternative centre of power. Thus, an authoritarian regime-building process, whether it follows revolutionary breakdown or regime breakdown is prone to use widespread repression against civil society actors.

In Egypt, state-led violence and repression increased after the ouster of Hosni Mubarak in 2011 and intensified even more following the 2013 coup d'état against the then elected president, Mohamed Morsi.[1] The regime has been adept at using widespread repression against all civil society actors, while intensifying and targeting repression against politicized civil society actors like human rights or political activists. Jordan, which did not foresee regime breakdown, is an example of an autocratizing regime, since it is an authoritarian regime that has been deepening its autocratic traits incrementally since the diffusion of demonstrations and uprisings in the Middle East and North Africa (MENA) in 2010/11.

---

[1] This will be further discussed in Chapter 4.

Repression, Targets of Repression and Dissent

As defined in the introduction, repression is the actual use or threat of the use of physical force against an individual or an organization within a state, intended to impose a cost on the target and to deter some activities or beliefs that are perceived to be challenging to a regime, government or institution (Goldstein 1978, in Davenport 2007, 2). This includes coercive strategies by the regime to influence the population within their territory through various means, whether covert or overt, whether through violent or nonviolent means (Davenport 2007, 3). Repression is the ruling elite's attempt to contain all challenges to its own rule through limiting opposition, and also through suppressing any political challenge that might erupt from the general population (Josua and Edel 2015). Acts of repression include imprisonment, disappearances, arrests, killing, and exiling, in addition to physical harm. They also include non-physical harm such as intimidation, surveillance, and restrictions on employment and/or on developing career opportunities (Josua and Edel 2015). In addition, repression can be:

> any policy taken by the state which limits the freedom of citizens to express discontent or which imposes costs upon those who do. Costs may be actively imposed or can merely be threatened. Repression is not simply switched on or off: it ranges widely in intensity, both across states and within states over time.
> **(Licht and Allen 2018, 484)**

A regime can use different forms of violence. These forms are mainly conceptualized as coercion, which is the use of force by the state's coercive apparatus, primarily police and military. Regimes can use direct forms of repression through coercion by inflicting physical harm on individuals. Yet they can also increase the cost of contentious activism through other means, mainly channelling, which 'is an indirect form of repression that seeks to deflect popular discontent and mitigate effective mobilization by managing dissent' (Heuer and Hierman 2022, 241). Here, protest is shaped rather than controlled (Earl 2011). Regimes sometimes choose to make their coercive actions visible to their populations through building their credibility and willingness to use force against dissent or wrongdoers. This is to pre-empt dissent in the future. Repression is mostly used against actors that might pose a challenge to the regime's existence (Licht and Allen 2018; Wintrobe 1998; Davenport 2007; Ritter 2014). Physical repression is the most common type of repression and is the strategy most feared by the opposition. It is primarily utilized to demobilize society as a whole (Nugent 2020; Bellin 2012).

Repression increases significantly during the first few months following an authoritarian regime transition, especially for those regimes that come to power through coups d'état or after the breakdown of their predecessor. In the uncertainty accompanying a leadership transition, new leaders concentrate on the development of their own reputation in the polity. They rely on coercion to build their reputation for 'toughness' in an effort to protect their nascent position in power and to deter hostile challenges in the future (Licht and Allen 2018, 583). Reputation-building becomes important for new leaders, especially those who did not have roles in the previous regime. Newly emerging regimes want to prevent citizens from engaging in protest activities and dissent. Repressive measures against oppositional groups and actors who might threaten the regime are an important strategy, not only for activists but also for citizens in general, to show which activities are permissible and which are not. This 'informs those not directly targeted about what is and is not deemed acceptable' within the confines of the new regime (Davenport and Loyle 2012, 81). Hence the political attitudes and behaviour of citizens at large become the target of repression. 'Techniques of punishment like repression are less about behavioral regulation than about protecting specific political-economic relations' (Davenport and Loyle 2012). Regimes can also use repression to increase their citizens' support for their rule. When regimes repress certain groups that are perceived by the public to be dangerous or 'terrorists', authoritarian regimes gain legitimacy from other groups in society, especially those who believe in this threat. In military regimes, which have the capacity to control coercive institutions, violence and repression become important factors in building a new support base, whereby the regime claims to be protecting the rest of society from different threats (Lachapelle 2022).

The longer an authoritarian regime stays in power, the more likely it is that it will limit the extent to which repression is utilized. Regimes that have undergone ruler change and smooth transition do not use excessive violence against citizens.

> Heirs to power, then, have political ties to the prior regime and enter through a smooth transfer of power. The incentive to repress for reputation-building is strongest for leaders that break with the prior regime, either through a legal process that ushers in the opposition or through an irregular turnover.
> **(Licht and Allen 2018, 586)**

Sometimes regimes want to be subtle and not show their repression in public. In some instances, repression intensifies through the use of different tactics of repression which are not coercive and not visible to the public. Yet these tactics are still designed to increase the costs of dissent, while upholding a regime's hold on power. In these cases, channelling does not silence dissent; instead, it channels it to other forms and avenues of opposition, which is developing institutional barriers to opposition (Heuer and Hierman 2022).

To limit civil society in the polity, authoritarian rulers rely on various types of repression. They censor and harass independent civil society actors, independent media, and political opponents, and weaken electoral bodies and institutions (Lührmann and Lindberg 2018). They use a range of complex methods to influence, control, and co-opt civil society actors, to end the autonomy of independent voices in the public sphere (Froissart 2014; Gilbert and Mohseni 2018; Greskovits 2015; Gerő and Kopper 2013; Kover 2015). In Turkey under Erdogan, for instance, organizations which have supported the regime have been widely tolerated, while those that have been more critical have been undermined (Doyle 2016, 2017). In Russia, foreign-funded or politically active civil society organizations have faced restrictive legal measures (Cheskin and March 2015). In addition, the Russian regime institutionalizes cooperation with selected civil society actors to hegemonize the public sphere. This is combined with an increase in legal and administrative procedures to control and limit the work of civil society (Daucé 2014).

In Egypt, we can see that in the eight years following the ouster of Morsi, the regime of Abdel-Fattah El-Sisi still uses excessive violence, both widespread and targeted, while in Jordan, a smooth transition occurred between the late King Hussein and his successor, King Abdullah II. However, in the few months following demonstrations in Jordan in 2011, and again when an attempted palace coup occurred in 2021, the regime increased its repressive tactics for a short time, primarily in the form of targeted repression. According to Nugent (2020), modern authoritarian regimes rely on selective repression but choose different strategies for different cases. For instance, they can utilize targeted repression to fend off oppositional mobilization for a while, especially at the start of their tenure in office, and can later vary the form of repression to limit dissent, such as shutting down independent media and targeting individual opposition leaders through extrajudicial means. Nugent argues that targeted repression in Egypt under the Mubarak regime was able to divide the political opposition, fragment it, and undermine its various identities. Although her analysis does not include Jordan, this process can also be discerned in Jordan after 2011. In Egypt, however, the Sisi regime has expanded the targeted repression of its predecessor into widespread repression.

The literature on repression mostly assumes that it is targeted against actors perceived to be a threat by the regime, as in Turkey and Russia. This reasoning is also applicable to Jordan, as is discussed in the coming chapters. However, it cannot explain the case of Egypt, where repression is rampant and has been institutionalized by the regime through the promulgation of repressive laws against civil society.

Widespread versus Targeted Repression and Dissent

While the majority of the literature does not distinguish between widespread and targeted repression, a burgeoning literature is emerging on making distinctions between the two types of repressive strategies.[2] Selective repression refers to a strategy in which a regime directs its coercion against a small number of opposition leaders or core activists. Widespread repression, on the other hand, is targeted against a wider number of citizens, without distinguishing whether they are in support of the regime, sympathize with the regime, or are just bystanders during certain contentious events (Hafez 2003; Demirel-Pegg and Rasler 2017). Widespread repression is 'collective targeting', while targeted repression is aimed at certain individuals (Demirel-Pegg and Rasler 2017).

Repression increases when a regime faces an increasing level of political threat from societal opposition (Regan and Henderson 2002). In this case, repertoires of dissent by the opposition or by civil society actors should also be taken into consideration. Regimes have different forms of responses to different forms of dissent (Earl, Soule, and McCarthy 2003). Scholars have identified two mechanisms: the first is the regime's decision to repress, and the second is the regime's choice of how much repression should be utilized. In this sense, the decision to repress and the reaction to repression are not the same. According to Ritter (2014), when a regime is stable, it is less likely to use widespread repression, yet when this stability is threatened by dissent, widespread repression can ensue (deMeritt 2016). Repression is mostly used as a pre-emptive strike against dissent by different regimes. The use of repression and violence against citizens impacts citizens' memories and their capacity and ability to dissent. When analysing repression and violence in Syria for instance, Ismail (2018) contends that regime violence against Syrians has impacted their memories and shaped their own understanding of their experiences with violence to different degrees. She argues that '[t]rough bodily and spatial inscriptions, subjects are instructed

---

[2] This idea expands on my previous work 'Mobilization, repression and policy concessions in authoritarian regimes: The cases of Egypt and Jordan'. *Political Studies* Online first https://journals.sagepub.com/doi/abs/10.1177/00323217221141426.

and reminded of interdictions against engaging in particular conduct' (Ismail 2018, 24).

In newly established authoritarian regimes, repression is typically used in the early stages of regime-building. For example, in Burma in the 1960s, after three months in power, the military repressed student protests on Rangoon University campus and outside of campus. The regime's response was mass, widespread repression against all students on campus, and the military opened fire against demonstrators. Even though this repressive episode was targeted at university students in particular, it was capable of eliminating and pre-empting dissent for twenty years (Boudreau 2009). While Boudreau (2009) argues that only targeted repression was used by the newly established regimes of Burma, Indonesia, and the Philippines in the 1960s, his analysis looks only at how these regimes have targeted 'political' opposition, without analysing the wider picture of regime repression against other civil society actors. The analysis does not discuss how coercion and repression were also disseminated against the press, the media, and independent civil society actors who are not politically active. In Africa, regimes who came to power after decolonization have used widespread repression in the public sphere. In Mozambique for instance, widespread repression was utilized in the first few years after its independence in 1975. Widespread detentions, deaths, displacements, and forced relocation of hundreds of thousands of citizens occurred during the decolonizing period (Igreja 2010). Similarly in decolonizing states in general and in the MENA in particular, state making was marked with an excessive use of state violence, ranging from Ataturk's state development process in Turkey to Saudi Arabia's state development process. The use of repression and violence helped in shaping the state which ensued, especially on the subjects under its jurisdiction. Accordingly, the use of excessive repression and violence was 'both exemplary and sometimes demonstratively cruel—and helped to mold the very imagination of what that power could do to those who opposed it' (Tripp 2013, 21).

When a long-standing authoritarian regime faces a sudden internal stability threat (diffusion of protest, for instance), in addition to the possibility that its own citizens could mobilize and dissent further, the regime utilizes targeted repression against potential dissidents. In China, for instance, the Chinese Communist Party used two main approaches in Xinjiang against the Uighurs. The first strategy was policing, using intensive surveillance and policing-based intelligence on the population. The second strategy was detention to re-educate the Uighurs, since the regime believed that they posed an ideological and terrorist threat. 'Both forms of repression are preventive, and while they are complementary in many respects, they work via different pathways. Intelligence-based and technology-based policing seeks to target and pre-empt citizens' capacity to challenge the party-state, while re-education and "transformation through education" target their willingness to do so' (Greitens et al. 2019/20, 45). According to Xu (2021), digital surveillance helps a regime to identify its radical opponents and thus use targeted repression against them, while at the same time co-opting the rest of the opposition. Selective repression takes place, when states direct their repression against a 'range of enemies' to neutralize their opposition (Demirel-Pegg and Rasler 2017; Hafez 2003). Demirel-Pegg and Rasler (2017) argue that widespread repression increases protest activities while targeted repression decreases it, through analysing the Gezi Park protests in Turkey. While this might be true at a certain protest event, it is not for a longer period of time, as in the case of Egypt.

Other studies point out that regime repression is used in cyclical forms and is mainly in response to possible dissent activities against the regime (Truex 2019). Pre-emptive repression may include imposing curfews, prohibiting any form of assembly, or imprisoning dissidents. It is argued that the detention of opposition figures precedes major national events in authoritarian regimes (Truex 2019). Here, targeted repression is utilized against the opposition, as argued by Truex (2019). Nevertheless, this is dependent on the regime in question and the regime's perception of the threat posed by dissent activities and public mobilization. Hence, as the case of Egypt demonstrates, mass detentions occur prior to certain times, as for instance in 2018 after an increase in Cairo metro ticket prices (Sika 2023) or prior to the anniversary of the 25 January uprising. Nevertheless, repression in the form of detention here is not targeted, but is diffused to passersby in downtown areas, or any civil society actor, irrespective of whether they are in the opposition or not.

Widespread repression and violence are costly, however, and can sometimes have an adverse effect by prompting further dissent and regime-threatening activities (Davenport 2007; Sika 2020). Authoritarian regimes therefore try to eliminate violence in the public sphere, while instantaneously eliminating their enemies. Targeted repression is when a regime identifies certain organizations or individuals as regime threatening and as a result chooses to eliminate this particular group or individual through different forms of violence like arrests, detentions, or killing (Gohdes 2020). This type of repression is the most frequently utilized and also the most preferred type of repression by autocrats (Xu 2021; Greitens 2016). Moreover, some scholars argue that when repression is targeted towards certain groups but not others, it is more effective in demobilization, since it is capable of dividing the opposition against one another (Nugent 2020). This strategy is important as a tool for pre-empting and eliminating all types of opposition activism against a certain regime (Demirel-Pegg and Rasler 2017). Targeted repression is typically used in long-standing authoritarian regimes with high state capacity. China, for instance, uses targeted repression against political opposition and potential political opposition through various forms of targeted violence, like targeting the families of opposition groups (Deng and O'Brien 2013), or imprisonment and detention of opposition actors (Noakes 2018). Other forms of targeted repression are also psychological. For instance, China 'operates through carefully tailored threats, emotional blackmail and pressure from people who are difficult to ignore', like family members, to change or inhibit an individual's protest potential (J.O'Brien and Deng 2017). In Saudi Arabia, activists who voice their dissent against the regime are targeted through different means of repression, mostly arrests and detention (Pan and Siegen 2019). In Belarus, targeted repression was utilized against the opposition in 2010–2011 after failed attempts to protest in favour of opposition presidential candidates. This targeted repression prevented further mobilization and opposition from being established (Vogel 2022). A decade after large mobilization processes were crushed, the year 2020 foresaw the largest public manifestation against Alexander Lukashenko, preceding the 2020 presidential election. When the protests intensified, widespread repression was utilized in addition to targeted repression. In other authoritarian regimes like Tanzania, Turkey, Uganda, and Russia, targeted repression is frequently utilized against the opposition, but also against certain subnational elites, who are charged with different criminal charges. In Russia, for instance, opposition mayors are more likely to be arrested for different criminal charges than other mayors (Buckley et al. 2022).

Conceptualizing Civil Society

There are several theoretical perspectives on civil society. From a liberal perspective, it is the arena outside the family, the state, and the market in which people develop interests for the enhancement of their community. Accordingly, free autonomous associations and independent organizations and unions are essential to maintain and increase social liberties within a given polity, and to limit the power of state actors (Putnam 1993; Howell and Pearce 2001; Fontana 2006). This positivist liberal tradition has been criticized by other scholars from leftist traditions, who argue that the line between the political and civil spheres is often blurred, with extensive political interventions in civil society, making the two spheres less independent and impartial than is assumed by the liberal tradition. From a more critical angle, the Marxist perspective perceives civil society to be embedded in a polity's power relations, intended to entrench the ruling class's power over the subaltern classes (Mercer 2002). For instance, some actors, like the Muslim Brotherhood in Egypt, Hamas in Palestine, and Hizbullah in Lebanon, are defined as social movements but have easily become part of the political sphere over the past two decades. Other entities have been established by government officials and have large memberships of civil servants. Syndicates and unions are also part of a corporatist structure, making them less independent and more reliant on their regimes (Härdig 2015; Bellin 2004).

Gramscian analysis perceives civil society as the space in which political and socioeconomic conflicts and struggles are performed. This is the space in which self-seeking competition for individual profit and for the market take place. It is divided into different groups and factions, with harmony more ideal than social reality (Fontana 2006). Civil society is not separated from politics but is rather a part of politics which is 'actively deployed' by the regime and by international donors, and which institutionalizes a regime's power (Gervasio and Teti 2020; Carapico 2002; Abdelrahman 2004). For Gramsci, the state is equal to political society and civil society and is 'hegemony protected by the armor of coercion' (Cospito 2018, 20). Civil society is thus a source of ideological influence but also of repression (Mayo 2011). In addition, civil society embodies the potential for social and political transformation and can be seen as a space where the state's hegemony over civil society is not complete. It constitutes an important site where existing values are challenged and new ones are established (Alagappa 2004, 29). It can 'develop a revolutionary strategy (a "war of position") that would be employed precisely in the arena of civil society, with the aim of disabling the coercive apparatus of the state, gaining access to political power, and creating the conditions that would give rise to a consensual society wherein no individual or group is reduced to a subaltern status' (Buttigieg 1995). Hegemony from this perspective is displaced in civil society, which represents a complex phenomenon of leadership and domination. It prevails when the majority of citizens accept the general direction that is imposed on social life by the dominant economic group, or by the political regime (Chalcraft 2016; Gramsci 1971, 12, in Chalcraft 2016, 30).

Looking at the Middle East, Chalcraft (2021) argues that a Gramscian analysis of civil society helps in understanding the Middle East through combining culture, society, and the state. He argues that Gramsci pays attention to the representation of social and political dynamics, in addition to the hierarchies of power and the historical context. Chalcraft further contends that the contradictions of civil society and its relations with the state can be understood through this analysis, as it demonstrates the power of the bourgeois capitalist order within a given state. It also enhances the ability of the state and ruling regime to receive their citizens' consent by diffusing 'bourgeois conceptions in civil society, buying off, co-opting, absorbing, diverting, and repressing revolutionary protest' (Chalcraft 2021, 90–91). Civil society is composed of different spaces, including all non-state organizations ranging from family to the media, but also to schools and religious institutions. Thus in certain instances, like education and religious institutions, the state can hegemonize and co-opt these organizations to spread its own ideas through creating ideas and ideologies around which society gathers (Salem 2020). In the 1950s Egypt for instance, where Naser was undergoing a regime-building process, consent was being built through education and media outlets, mainly the Voice of the Arabs radio station (Salem 2020).

Civil society can display both Gramscian and positivist liberal perspectives. It constitutes a 'realm of power, inequality, struggle and conflict among competing interests', which also comprises 'anti-democratic' actors. It can include some social interests that are exclusionary and illiberal in nature (Lorch 2021, 82; Härdig 2015). It is in civil society that regime power and coercion can be understood. How does a regime react to individuals who do not consent to the national narrative, language, and/or culture of the political society (Chalcraft 2016, 30)? It can be seen as a 'space where diverse actors engage both through contention and cooperation' (Härdig 2015, 1134). This is important analytically, but it also is important to understand how and why authoritarian regimes treat civil society actors differently during different times and spaces. When a regime has already been established and is upgrading its authoritarian institutions and autocratizing, it tolerates most civil society actors. It co-opts the tolerable opposition, dominates non-governmental organizations (NGOs), and is able to hegemonize the public sphere through blurring the line between the regime and non-state actors. Business associations become essential in this, since they uphold the power and interests of the authoritarian regime yet are also 'private' actors.

On the other hand, when a regime experiences breakdown, autocratization, and a transition to another autocratic regime, civil society becomes the arena of conflict. Instead of relying on the old order, under which certain civil society actors were present and dominated by the previous authoritarian regime, the autocratizing regime wants to establish a new consensus, new hegemony, and domination, and thus the use of violence, coercion, and widespread repression is imminent.

To understand the different dynamics and why regimes use widespread repression against civil society actors at times and targeted repression at others, I argue that the time and space in which an authoritarian regime is situated influence the development of political opportunities and threats within a given political context. The regime's perception of threat from civil society actors also plays a role in how it acts towards them. Authoritarian regimes undergoing regime-building after breakdown act and react differently towards civil society than long-standing authoritarian regimes, which develop different authoritarian 'upgrading measures' (Hinnebusch 2012). In the first group, especially those regimes that are established after the breakdown of their predecessor, distrust between the regime and civil society is high; the regime's perception of threat from civil society is also high, and hence widespread repression is utilized.[3] Long-established authoritarian regimes, or those where the leadership has changed harmoniously without abrupt breakdown, build more consent and are able to hegemonize civil society through their existing authoritarian upgrading measures, increasing their co-optation strategies while limiting coercion to targeted repression against opposition actors (Edel and Josua 2018; Gerschewski 2013).

The Agency of Civil Society in Authoritarian Regimes

Within this understanding of civil society, we can focus on the cooperative ties which are developed between different CSOs, how these organizations are able to network together, and how they are integrated into different coalitions and networks. To understand social and political change in different regimes, we should not only analyse the number of CSOs, but we should also understand their properties and how they are linked to each other through different patterns. This makes our understanding more focused on 'collective action fields' (Diani 2015, 4). Analysing civil society as parts of collective action fields where networks and coalition partnerships are built helps us identify and understand how they act and react in different contexts (Diani 2015). Under authoritarian regimes, these interactions and partnerships are not easily established. Civil society actors tend to moderate their civic and political participation and to change relational patterns from networking to

---

[3] This is similar to Levitsky and Way's (2013) argument about the durability of revolutionary regimes that develop certain strategies, such as the destruction of independent power centres and the development of strong ruling parties, and which enhance their coercive capacity. However, I focus here on civil society actors in particular in order to understand how consent and coercion differ in various authoritarian regimes.

coalition-building in order to ensure their work and presence in the public sphere. 'In repressive contexts, community-based resistance has often proved more feasible and effective than open challenges conducted through coalitions and movements. Moreover, forms of resistance do not necessarily overlap with the political, and a great deal of attention must thus be given to "infrapolitical practices"' (Diani 2015, 209).

In the MENA, the 2011 uprisings were important in highlighting the different repertoires of contentions and performances that have developed throughout the preceding years and decades. In Egypt for instance, the ability of activists to mobilize for demonstrations can better be grasped through understanding the previous decade's movements' repertoires of contention, and how they resonated with society at large (Tripp 2013).

Authoritarian Regime-Building and Civil Society

After regime breakdown, an autocratizing regime targets civil society actors as a first strategy, while simultaneously cracking down on civil and political freedoms in general (Cassani and Tomini 2019). Different strategies are used against these actors, such as developing new discourses and narratives which delegitimize critical voices in civil society while also polarizing some actors. There is a systematic attack on independent voices (Kover 2015). Autocratizing regimes that transition after breakdown also pass laws hampering the work of civil society, while restricting public and political debates. Policies are changed to allocate public funds to actors willing to be co-opted by the emergent regime. They then develop a discourse of 'good' versus 'bad' civil society actors, which further polarizes them within the regime (Van Til 2015). Stigma and criminal labelling are used to discredit and stifle civil society work and particular actors who might pose a threat to the new autocratizing regime. Labelling opposition groups or civil society actors as committing espionage is another important tactic of control, as are passing emergency laws and stripping national councils of their powers. Another important strategy is using intimidation to obstruct the work of independent civil society actors and the infiltration of civil society organizations by security personnel (Borgh and Terwindt 2012).

An interesting example of authoritarian state-building can be seen in Belarus. Lukashenko came to power in 1994, at a time when civil society organizations and independent media were flourishing after the fall of the Soviet Union. He won electoral victories and referendums that strengthened his power over the executive, while at the same time increasing coercion against his opponents (Wilson 2011). By 2001, he had consolidated his power and hegemony over the regime. He developed a discourse against the opposition in which he articulated 'anti-corruption' and advocated for an economic reform process that would increase the role of the state in the economy. His economic policies were highly popular among the masses, but their effect was to redefine Belarusian national identity (Tantidis 2021; Way 2015).

A new regime's linkage with various actors in the international community also impacts the way in which it deals with civil society actors. In the case of Belarus, Lukashenko strengthened his ties to Russia. He developed his personal image as a strongman who could protect Belarus from any external threat (Tantidis 2021). He weakened civil society organizations through strict registration procedures, increasing fines on those who did not comply with state regulations, and imposing tax audits. Judges who refused to carry out these orders were either dismissed or subjected to disciplinary procedures. While doing so, Lukashenko increased repression against civil society actors, and opposition activists and journalists were subject to disappearances and indiscriminate detention (Way 2015; Tantidis 2021, 16). He succeeded in limiting the independence and autonomy of civil society actors, which ultimately helped to stifle the development of civil society and political opposition. In other emerging authoritarian and hybrid regimes, it has been found that strong linkages with autocratic actors like China and Russia has been a significant predictor for the establishment of legal barriers against civil society in these regimes (Gilbert and Payam 2018). Linkages with Western democratic regimes can also have negative impacts on the development of civil society in authoritarian regimes. When Western allies, like the United States for instance support their authoritarian allies, even when these regimes conduct grave human rights atrocities, Western allies can indirectly help in crushing civil society actors and the political opposition. This can be in the form of arms sales or in the form of helping the coercive institutions like the use of the police and military through direct and indirect aid (Yom 2016).

Authoritarian Regime Continuity and Civil Society

In this study, I build on this debate by arguing that civil society can include elements of the positivist liberal perspective of change towards democracy, as well as elements of Gramscian perspectives on regime domination and hegemony. Civil society organizations can increase their members' social capital, especially their ability to form networks of trust among rival actors. They are also capable of building a strong and coherent civil society, which can contest the legitimacy of the regime in various ways.[4] In the Middle East, for instance, the first decade of the twenty-first century is full of examples where historical rivals such as Islamists and Marxists bridged their differences and developed various protest movements to oppose their regimes. In Egypt in 2004, for example, Islamists, liberals, and Marxists developed a network, the Kifaya movement, against the Mubarak regime.[5] However, civil society can also be infiltrated by the regime and become another arm prolonging its endurance. If this happens, actors striving for social and political power are empowered in this space. Moreover, the authoritarian regime itself develops certain rules to halt the functioning of civil society (Jamal 2009; Carapico 2013; Sika 2019).

As a result, civil society can be both an actor of change and an actor of resilience within an authoritarian regime. Hence, authoritarian regimes seek to control all types of civil society, to ensure their own dominance and hegemony in the polity. Accordingly, a long-standing authoritarian regime uses different authoritarian strategies towards civil society actors. The authoritarian regime here wants to limit coercion to ensure that it does not backfire, and thus more co-optation of civil society actors occurs, while limiting repression to oppositional civil society actors who are not co-optable or who pose a political threat to the regime's existence (Greitens 2016; Xu 2021).

Some empirical evidence suggests that civil society's contribution to democratization has been limited (Doyle 2017). In the MENA, this trend has been occurring, where it has been shown that civil society organizations can in fact assist in embedding authoritarian regimes (Kamrava and Mora 1998; Berman 1997; Jamal 2009; Cavatrota and Durac 2011). Some studies have gone as far as to argue that civil society in MENA helps to sustain and extend state power in the polity. In Jordan, for instance, civil society facilitates the monitoring of activism (Doyle 2017). In such cases, regimes facilitate restrictive legal measures to eliminate the presence of organizations that could pose an existential threat to them. Collective action by activists and protest movements have also been carefully monitored to control mobilization (Doyle 2017).

The authoritarian measures and practices employed by authoritarian leaders against civil society actors are a major reason why civil society actors are closely tied to these regimes and embed their power and authority. These actors have to ensure that their work does not cross certain red lines, and in order to continue operating in different areas of concern, like development,

---

[4] For more discussions on social capital see Putnam; Bourdieu; Jamal.
[5] For more discussions on this see Dina Shehata; Audet al-Siyassa; Rabab El Mahdi Enough; and Nadine Sika 'Youth Activism'.

they need to rely on patronage networks developed by the regime itself. 'If they conform then they can operate, be effective and increase social capital. However, if they refuse to play by the "corrupt" rules of the game, they can be shut down, ostracized and become ineffective, losing social capital as a consequence' (Durac and Cavatorta 2015, 177). Organizations associated with the regime or that play by the rules of the authoritarian game are tolerated, while other organizations which do not conform to the rules are outlawed and face various legal and practical problems to prevent them from working effectively for their cause. For instance, legislation that 'severely restricts civil society organizations, state closure of CSOs [civil society organizations], and also the creation of "state friendly" CSOs or government-backed "non-governmental" organizations (GONGOs) to replace independent CSOs' (Doyle 2017, 248) is often the rule in authoritarian regimes.

Civil society actors are also often co-opted by an authoritarian regime through their integration into interest groups or corporatist arrangements. Authoritarian regimes sometimes even establish mass organizations to incorporate civil society actors or utilize personal relationships and patronage systems to control them (Lorch and Bunk 2017).

Civil society can even be useful for authoritarian regimes in helping to reduce social inequalities. Through their linkage with the regime and their networking capability with other voluntary organizations, they can build collaboration among different actors to help develop the economic and social development projects of a given regime. Their networks can also utilize mobilizational and indoctrination policies introduced by the regime to sustain the status quo (Bernhard et al. 2017, 298).[6] This cooperative strategy can be seen in the case of Jordan, for instance, whereas in Egypt the regime has increased its coercion against both friends and foes alike and has cracked down on all types of civil society organizations, irrespective of whether they are for or against the regime.

Civil society has also been used as a legitimation strategy by authoritarian regimes (Lorch and Bunk 2017). For instance, the presence of civil society provides a democratic façade both internally for the citizens at large and externally for the international community. Making civil society actors play by the rules entrenches bureaucratic practices within a given regime and 'constantly reaffirms the existing, authoritarian order' (Lorch and Bunk 2017, 990). In addition, consulting civil society actors on various matters familiarizes these regimes with the most pressing social demands, and it can adapt

---

[6] For more discussion on this see Ekrem Karakoç. 2017. 'A theory of redistribution in new democracies: Income disparity in new democracies in Europe'. *Comparative Politics* 49 (3): 311–330.

accordingly. Lastly, civil society actors who work mainly in the welfare sector fulfil social needs and hence decrease the capacity gap in the economy (Lorch and Bunk 2017).

Civil society in authoritarian settings in South-East Asia, for instance, can exhibit socially exclusionary and illiberal traits which hinder democratization and can augment the power of an authoritarian regime. Civil society actors in some cases can align themselves with different authoritarian political camps, which contributes not only to authoritarian resilience but also to democratic regression in weak democracies (Lorch 2021).

The Consequences of International Support for Civil Society in Authoritarian Regimes

When analysing civil society actors and the space in which they function, it is important to examine the role of international actors in supporting civil society. With the rise of neoliberalism worldwide in the 1990s and the democratization processes in Latin America and Eastern and Central Europe, the international community, and especially Western governments, have supported the work of independent civil society in many countries, especially in the Global South. This has been directed towards the establishment of both development and charitable initiatives and, supposedly, the democratizing of authoritarian regimes.

Although restrictions on civil society actors have always existed, the last decade has witnessed a surge in these attacks, hand in hand with the rising tide of autocratization and democratic backsliding (Buyse 2018; Lührmann et.al. 2018). Another important aspect is that international support for civil society actors in the form of foreign funds has also been decreasing. Both domestic and international factors account for the shrinking space for civil society work (Poppe and Wolff 2017). Recent research analysing ninety-eight low-and middle-income countries worldwide found that fifty-one of them have either restricted or prohibited foreign funding to civil society actors (Christensen and Weinstein 2013; Poppe and Wolff 2017). Restricting foreign aid is an expression of a regime's perception of foreign funding as supporting instability or empowering civil society actors to mobilize against its control. 'Worries about international retaliation can, however, retrain such governments if they come to fear that clamping down will cost them more than it is worth' (Christensen and Weinstein 2013, 79). It is clear, however, that in certain cases which are politically and strategically important for Western democracy promotion donors, as are many countries in MENA, minimal effort is exerted by the funding bodies against these restrictions. Nevertheless, the problem with such support lies in the fact that the European Union and the United States have prioritized stability over the promotion of democracy, human rights and freedoms, and have hence consistently supported authoritarian regimes (Teti et al. 2020).

Support for civil society from Western democracies has been challenging for two main reasons. The first is that Arab regimes have accepted development aid as a form of assistance for their own development projects, and in so far as governments are involved in state and civil society partnerships, the donors have targeted development and charity. Other projects, especially concerning human rights or freedoms, have not been accepted by Arab regimes (Carapico 2002; Carapico 2013). These regimes have used a discourse of suspicion towards human rights activists who receive their funding from Western nations. Suspicion of Western-affiliated organizations has been apparent, human rights activists have been imprisoned, and after the Arab uprisings of 2011 these activists were attacked as 'foreign agents' working against the national interest or for the West. In the meantime, Western nations have supported these autocratic regimes in the interests of stability, and do not ask for democratization or pressure for political reform for fear of increasing migration from those countries to the West. In other authoritarian regimes, foreign-funded NGOs are referred to as 'foreign agents'. Ethiopia, for instance, has banned organizations working on freedom and human rights issues. In addition, any organization that receives more than 10% of its funding from abroad is also prohibited. Similarly, in Azerbaijan and Uzbekistan, foreign-funded organizations have been physically and verbally attacked, as well as criminalized by these regimes and their adherents (Buyse 2018). Repression against civil society actors is hence politicized but has also become more subtle over the past decade. Autocrats have learned to accuse civil society actors of being foreign agents who have ulterior motives against their home country (Miles and Croucher 2013). In the case of autocratization processes after authoritarian breakdown, as the Egyptian case study will demonstrate later in the book, these policies are accentuated and are used by the regime as a legitimate reason for increasing repression against civil society actors who receive foreign funding.

Another aspect of foreign support holds an important consequence which is that these Western alliances support and help authoritarian rulers in the region to suppress opposition, through providing them with the coercive strategies and fiscal means to support the incumbent rulers. They help in establishing a large number of civil society actors that work in the development sector, through advancing private-public partnerships. However, they provide minimal support for the opposition. Another form of support is developed through military aid, which improves the regime's ability to control their territory, but also increases the coercive capacity of the police force and the military's capacity to repress opposition (Yom 2016).

Another important hindrance to the support of civil society in authoritarian regimes is the 'terrorism' label. Many authoritarian regimes utilize this accusation to crack down on various organizations, demonstrating that they are 'terrorists' and can threaten stability. The so-called war on terror has negatively affected civil society. The vague language accompanying mandates against terrorism leads to more coercion against civil society actors who are critical of the regime (Borgh and Terwindt 2012, 1067). This tool is essential in autocratizing regimes as well, since the label of 'terrorism' has been accentuated and also provided the regime with legitimacy to increase repression. In Egypt, for instance, the Muslim Brotherhood have been labelled as a 'terrorist organization' since 2013. Hence, the regime represses any business or charity organization, hospital, or school that is associated with the Brotherhood and justifies this repression due to their 'terrorist' nature.

Conclusion

This chapter situated the major debates on repression, its different forms, and the extent to which it increases, is sometimes used diffusely, and is targeted at others, within the burgeoning literature on autocratization. It argues that a nuanced analysis of why different types of repressive strategies occur in different authoritarian regimes sheds light on the different repertoires of repression employed by the regimes in question. It also demonstrates that these repressive repertoires influence why and how civil society actors respond to different types of repression. Accordingly, the starting point of a regime and its perception of threat from civil society actors should take the recent historical experiences of the authoritarian regime into consideration, whether the regime has experienced breakdown or is a resilient authoritarian regime. Following the conceptualization of repression, and how and why it is employed differently in authoritarian regimes, a conceptualization of civil society is developed. Here, civil society is analysed as a contested and cooperative space between an authoritarian regime on the one hand and societal actors on the other. It shows how civil society is a space in which authoritarian regimes try to dominate and hegemonize society, and where opposition forces are also trying to develop counter-hegemonies to influence the public sphere. Depending on how the regime perceives civil society and whether it perceives civil society as a threat to its existence or whether it sees it as an opportunity for hegemony and domination, repression, and/or co-optation ensue. In newly established authoritarian regimes, where the regime is still being established, more repression and coercion are directed at all civil society actors, while targeting the opposition, in an effort to build the regime's reputation for ferocity, and to build consent through hegemonizing the public sphere. In older, established regimes which do not face imminent threats to their existence, and which have already upgraded their authoritarian strategies, more co-optation than repression is used in dealing with civil society.

The following chapters will apply these conceptual analyses of repression and civil society to the authoritarian regimes of Egypt and Jordan. Chapters 2 and 3 will discuss why and how widespread repression is utilized in the case of Egypt, relying on the repression–dissent model in social movement studies. It will also draw on the political context of authoritarian regime breakdown and autocratization and how this increases repression, and how civil society actors develop their repertoires of contention in response. Chapters 4 and 5, on the other hand, will discuss why and how targeted repression is utilized in the case of Jordan, relying on the concession–repression literature. It will also draw on the political context of authoritarian regime resilience and how this influences both regimes' repertoires of suppression and activists' repertoires of contention.

Bibliography

Abdelrahman, Maha. 2002. 'The politics of "uncivil" society in Egypt'. *Review of African Political Economy* 29 (91): 21–35.

Abdelrahman, Maha. 2004. *Civil Society Exposed: The Politics of NGOs in Egypt*. Cairo: The American University Press.

Alagappa, Muthiah, ed. 2004. *Civil Society and Political Change in Asia: Explanding and Contracting Democratic Space*. Stanford: Stanford University Press.

al-Anani, Khalil. 2020. 'Devout neoliberalism?! Explaining Egypt's Muslim Brotherhood's socio-economic perspective and policies'. *Politics and Religion* 13: 748–767.

Alexander, Jeffery. 2006. *The Civil Sphere*. Oxford: Oxford University Press.

Al-Naggar, Gamal Abdel Hay, Hanan Abdallah Abdel Samad, and Yosry Mohamed Salem Habak. 2016. 'Mu'alajat al-sohof al-misriyya le anshitat munazamat al-mujtama' al-madani [The representation of civil society organizations in Egyptian Print Media]'. *Majalat buhouth al-tarbiyya al-naw'iyya* 41: 364–424. https://mbse.journals.ekb.eg/article_139748_0b259d6044a5ed87c5daabd41518f28e.pdf

al-Sayyid, Mustapha. 1993. 'A civil society in Egypt?' *The Middle East Journal* 47 (2): 228–242.

Al-Sayyid, Mustapha. 1995. 'The concept of civil society and the Arab world'. In *Political Liberalization and Democratization in the Arab World*, vol. 1, by Rex Brynen, Bahgat Korany, and Paul Noble, 131–147. Lynne Rienner.

Atalay, Zeynep. 2016. 'Vernacularization of liberal civil society by transnational Islamist NGO networks'. *Global Networks* 16 (3): 1470–2266.

Bayat, Asef. 2013. 'Post-Islamism at large'. In *Post-Islamism: The Changing Faces of Political Islam*, by Asef Bayat, 3–34. Oxford: Oxford University Press.

Bellin, Eva. 2004. 'The robustness of authoritarianism in the Middle East: Exceptionalism in comparative perspective'. *Comparative Politics* 36 (2): 139–157.

Bellin, Eva. 2012. 'Reconsidering authoritarianism in the Arab World'. *Comparative Politics* 44 (2): 127–149.

Berman, Sheri. 1997. 'Civil society and political instituionalization'. *American Behavioral Scientist* 40 (5): 562–574. https://doi.org/10.1177/0002764297040005003

Bernhard, Michael, Tiago Fernandes, and Rui Branco. 2017. 'Introduction: Civil society and democracy in an era of inequality'. *Comparative Politics* 49 (3): 297–309.

Borgh, Chris van der and Carolijn Terwindt. 2012. 'Shrinking operational space of NGOs—a framework of analysis'. *Development in Practice* 22 (8): 1065–1081.

Boudreau, Vince. 2009. *Resisting Dictatorship: Repression and Protest in Southeast Asia*. Cambridge: Cambridge University Press.

Boulkaibet, Ahlem. 2021. 'Da'f al-mujta'a al-madany fy al-'alam al-'araby: al-asbab wa al-ma'aalat [The weakness of civil society in the Arab World: Causes and prospects]'. *Majalet al-m'iar* 25 (56): 761–773.

Buckley, Noah, Ora John Reuter, Michael Rochlitz, and Anton Aisin. 2022. 'Staying out of trouble: Criminal cases against Russian mayors'. *Comparative Political Studies* 55 (9): 1539–1568.

Buttigieg, Joseph. 1995. 'Gramsci on civil society'. *Boundary* 2 (3): 1032.

Buyse, Antoine. 2018. 'Squeezing civic space: Restrictions on civil society organizations and the linkages with human rights'. *The International Journal of Human Rights* 22 (8): 966–988.

Carapico, Sheila. 2002. 'Foreign aid for promoting democracy in the Arab world'. *The Middle East Journal* 56 (3): 379–395.

Carapico, Sheila. 2013. *Political Aid and Arab Activism: Democracy Promotion, Justice and Representation*. Cambridge: Cambridge University Press.

Cassani, Andrea and Luca Tomini. 2019. *Autocratization in Post-Cold War Political Regimes*. Houndmills: Palgrave Macmillan.

Cavatorta, Francesco and Vincent Durac. 2011. Civil Society and Democratization in the Arab World: The Dynamics of Activism. London: Routledge.

Chalcraft, John. 2016. *Popular Politics in the Making of the Modern Middle East*. Cambridge: Cambridge University Press.

Chalcraft, John. 2021. 'Middle East popular politics in Gramscian perspective'. *Comparative Studies of South Asia, Africa and the Middle East* 41 (3): 469–484.

Chalcraft, John. 2021. 'Revolutionary weakness in Gramscian perspective: The Arab Middle East and North Africa since 2011'. *Middle East Critique* 30 (1): 87–104.

Cheskin, Ammon and Luke March. 2015. 'State–society relations in contemporary Russia: New forms of political and social contention'. *East European Politics* 31 (3): 261–273.

Christensen, Darin and Jeremy Weinstein. 2013. 'Defunding dissent: Restrictions on aid to NGOs'. *Journal of Democracy* 24 (2): 77–91.

Clark, Janine. 2012. 'Patronage, prestige, and power: The Islamic Center Charity Society's political role within the Muslim Brotherhood'. In *Islamist Politics in the Middle East: Movements and Change*, by Samer Shehata, 68–88. London: Routledge.

Cospito, Giuseppe. 2018. 'Dizionario gramsciano/Gramsci dictionary: Hegemony'. *International Gramsci Journal* 3 (1): 18–25.

Daucé, Françoise. 2014. 'The government and human rights groups in Russia: Civilized oppression?' *Journal of Civil Society* 10 (3): 239–254 DOI: 10.1080/17448689.2014.941087

Davenport, Christian. 2007. 'State repression and political order'. *Annual Review of Political Science* 10 (1): 1–23.

Davenport, Christian and Cyanne Loyle. 2012. 'The states must be crazy: Dissent and the puzzle of repressive persistence'. *International Journal of Conflict and Violence* 6 (1): 76–95.

Della Porta, Donatella. 2020. 'Building bridges: Social movements and civil society in times of crisis'. *Voluntas* 31: 938–948.

deMeritt, Jacqueline H. R. 2016. 'The strategic use of state repression and political violence'. *Oxford Research Encyclopedia of Politics* DOI: 10.1093/acrefore/9780190228637.013.32.

Demirel-Pegg, Tijen and Karen Rasler. 2017. 'Protesters Under the Gun: Under What Conditions do States Manage Backfire Effects Successfully'. *Annual Meeting of the International Studies Association.*

Deng, Yanhua and Kevin O'Brien. 2013. 'Relational repression in China: Using social ties to demobilize protesters'. *The China Quarterly* 215: 533–552.

Diani, Mario. 2015. *The Cement of Civil Society: Studying Networks in Localities*. Cambridge: Cambridge University Press.

Doyle, Jessica Leigh. 2016. 'Civil society as ideology in the Middle East: A critical perspective'. *British Journal of Middle Eastern Studies* 43 (3): 403–422 DOI: 10.1080/13530194.2015.1102713

Doyle, Jessica Leigh. 2017. 'State control of civil society organizations: The case of Turkey'. *Democratization* 24 (2): 244-264.

Durac, Vincent and Francesco Cavatorta. 2015. *Politics and Governance in the Middle East*. London: Palgrave.

Earl, Jennifer. 2011. 'Political repression: Iron fists, velvet gloves, and diffuse control'. *Annual Review of Sociology* 37: 261-284.

Earl, Jennifer, Sarah A Soule, and John McCarthy. 2003. 'Protest under fire? Explaining the policing of protest'. *American Sociological Review* 68 (4): 581-606.

Edel, Mirjam and Maria Josua. 2018. 'How authoritarian rulers seek to legitimize repression: Framing mass killings in Egypt and Uzbekistan'. *Democratization* 25 (5): 882-900.

Froissart, Chloe. 2014. 'The ambiguities between contention and political participation: A study of civil society development in authoritarian regimes'. *Journal of Civil Society* 10 (3): 219-222 DOI: 10.1080/17448689.2014.944758

Fontana, Bendetto. 2006. 'Liberty and domination: Civil society in Gramsci'. *Boundary 2: An International Journal of Literature and Culture* 33 (2): 50-74.

Fu, Diana and Greg Distelhorst. 2017. 'Grassroots participation and repression under Hu Jintao and Xi Jinping'. *The China Journal* (79): 100-122.

Gerő, Márton and Ákos Kopper. 2013. 'Fake and dishonest: Pathologies of differentiation of the civil and the political sphere in Hungary'. *Journal of Civil Society* 9 (4): 361-374 DOI: 10.1080/17448689.2013.844449

Gerschewski, Johannes. 2013. 'The three pillars of stability: Legitimation, repression, and co-optation in autocratic regimes'. *Democratization* 20 (1): 13-38.

Gervasio, Gennaro and Andrea Teti. 2020. 'Prelude to the revolution. Independent civic activists in Mubarak's Egypt and the quest for hegemony'. *Journal of North African Studies* 26 (6): 1099-1121.

Gilbert, Leah and Mohseni Payam. 2018. 'Disabling dissent: The colour revolutions, autocratic linkages, and civil society regulations in hybrid regimes'. *Contemporary Politics* 24 (4): 454-480.

Gohdes, Anita. 2020. 'Repression technology: Internet accessibility and state violence'. *American Journal of Political Science* 64 (3): 488-503.

Goldstein, Robert Justin. 1978. *Political Repression in Modern America: from 1870 to the Present*. Cambridge, MA: Schenkman.

Gramsci, Antonio. 1971. *Selections from the Prison Notebooks of Antonio Gramsci*. Ed. and trans. Quintin Hoare and Geoffrey Nowell Smith. London: Lawrence and Wishart.

Greitens, Sheena Chestnut. 2016. *Dictators and Their Secret Police: Coercive Institutions and State Violence*. Cambridge, MA: Cambridge University Press.

Greitens, Sheena Chestnut, Myunghee Lee, and Emir Yazici. 2019/20. 'Counterterrorism and preventive repression: China's changing strategy in Xinjiang'. *International Security* 44 (3): 9–47.

Greskovits, B. 2015. 'The hollowing and backsliding of democracy in East Central Europe'. *Global Policy* 6 (S1): 28–37.

Habermas, Jürgen. 1996. *Between Facts and Norms: Contributions to a Discourse Theory of Law and Democracy*. Cambridge: Polity Press.

Hafez, Mohammed M. 2003. *Why Muslims Rebel: Repression and Resistance in the Islamic World*. Boulder: Lynne Rienner.

Härdig, Anders. 2015. 'Beyond the Arab revolts: Conceptualizing civil society in the Middle East and North Africa'. *Democratization* 22 (6): 1131–1153.

Hellmeier, Sebastian, Rowan Cole, Sandra Grahn, Palina Kolvani, Jean Lachapelle, Anna Lührmann, et al. 2020. 'State of the world 2020: Autocratization turns viral'. *Democratization* 28 (6): 1053–1074.

Heuer, Vera and Brent Hierman. 2022. 'Manhandling and mediation: Unpacking the repressive repertoire in Kazakhstan's 2016 anti-land reform protests'. *Asian Security* 18 (3): 239–256.

Hinnebusch, Raymond. 2012. 'Syria: From "authoritarian upgrading" to revolution?' *International Affairs* 88 (1): 95–113.

Howell, Jude and Jenny Pearce. 2001. *Civil Society and Development: A Critical Exploration*. Boulder: Lynne Rienner.

Igreja, Victor. 2010. 'Frelimo's political ruling through violence and memory in postcolonial Mozambique'. *Journal of Southern African Studies* 36 (4): 781–799.

Ismail, Saloua. 2018. *The Rule of Violence: Subjectivity, Memory and Government in Syria*. Cambridge: Cambridge University Press.

Jamal, Amaney. 2009. *Barriers to Democracy*. Princeton: Princeton University Press.

Josua, Maria and Mirjam Edel. 2015. 'To repress or not to repress-regime survival strategies in the Arab Spring'. *Terrorism and Political Violence* 27 (2): 289–309.

J.O'Brien, Kevin and Yanhua Deng. 2017. 'Preventing protest one person at a time: Psychological coercion and relational repression in China'. *China Review* 17 (2): 179–201.

Lachapelle, Jean. 2022. 'Repression reconsidered: Bystander effects and legitimation in authoritarian regimes'. *Comparative Politics* DOI: 10.5129/001041522X16317396828722.

Lachpelle, Jean, Steven Levitsky, Lucan A. Way, and Adam E. Casey. 2020. 'Social revolution and authoritarian durability'. *World Politics* 72 (4): 557–600.

Landau, Ingrid. 2008. 'Law and civil society in Cambodia and Vietnam: A Gramscian perspective'. *Journal of Contemporary Asia* 38 (2): 244–258.

Levitsky, Steven and Lucan Way. 2013. 'The durability of revolutionary regimes'. *Journal of Democracy* 24 (3): 5–17.

Licht, Amanda and Susan Hannah Allen. 2018. 'Repressing for reputation: Leadership transitions, uncertainty, and the repression of domestic populations'. *Journal of Peace Research* 55 (5): 582–595.

Lorch, Jasmin. 2021. 'Elite capture, civil society and democratic backsliding in Bangladesh, Thailand and the Philippines'. *Democratization* 28 (1): 81–102.

Lorch, Jasmin and Bettina Bunk. 2017. 'Using civil society as an authoritarian legitimation strategy: Algeria and Mozambique in comparative perspective'. *Democratizaiton* 24 (6): 987–1005.

Lührmann, Anna et.al. 2018. 'State of the world 2017: Autoratization and exlusion?' *Demoratization* 25 (8): 1321–1340. https://doi.org/10.1080/13510347.2018.1479693

Lührmann, Anna, and Staffan Lindberg. 2018. 'A third wave of autocratization is here: What is new about it?' *Democratization* 26 (7): 1095–1113.

Lührmann, Anna and Staffan Lindberg. 2019. 'A third wave of autocratization is here: What is new about it?' *Democratization* 26 (7): 1095–1113.

Kamrava, Mehran and Frank Mora. 1998. 'Civil society and democratisation in comparative perspective: Latin America and the Middle East'. *Third World Quarterly* 19 (5): 893–915.

Kover, Agnes. 2015. 'Captured by state and church: Concerns about civil society in democratic Hungary'. *Nonprofit Policy Forum* 6 (2): 187–212. https://doi.org/10.1515/npf-2014-0010.

Mayo, Peter. 2011. 'The centrality of the state in neoliberal times'. *International Gramsci Journal* 1 (3): 57–71.

Mercer, Claire. 2002. 'NGOs, civil society and democratization: A critical review of the literature'. *Progress in Development Studies* 2 (1): 5–22.

Miles, Lilian and Richard Croucher. 2013. 'Gramsci, counter-hegemony and labour union–civil society organisation coalitions in Malaysia'. *Journal of Contemporary Asia* 43 (3): 413–427.

Mirshak, Nadim. 2019. 'Rethinking resistance under authoritarianism: Civil society and non-contentious forms of contestation in post-uprisings Egypt'. *Social Movement Studies* 18 (6): 702–719.

Newman, Edward. 2013. 'State building in historical perspective: Implications for peacebuilding'. *Peacebuilding* 1 (1): 141–157.

Noakes, Stephen. 2018. 'A disappearing act: The evolution of China's administrative detention system'. *Journal of Chinese Political Science* (23): 199–216.

Nugent, Elizabeth. 2020. *After Repression: How Polarization Derails Democratic Transition*. Princeton: Princeton University Press.

Pan, Jennifer and Alexander Siegen. 2019. 'How Saudi crackdowns fail to silence online dissent'. *American Political Science Review* 114 (1): 109–125.

Pelke, Lars and Aurel Croissant. 2021. 'Conceptualizing and measuring autocratization episodes'. *Swiss Political Science Review* 27 (2): 434–448.

Poppe, Annika Elena and Jonas Wolff. 2017. 'The contested spaces of civil society in a plural world: Norm contestation in the debate about restrictions on international civil society support'. *Contemporary Politics* 23 (4): 469–488.

Putnam, Robert. 1993. *Making Democracy Work: Civic Traditions in Modern Italy*. NJ: Princeton University Press.

Regan, Patrick M. and Errol A. Henderson. 2002. 'Democracy, threats and political repression in developing countries: Are democracies internally less violent?' *Third World Quarterly* 23 (1): 119–136.

Ritter, Emily Hencken. 2014. 'Policy disputes, political survival, and the onset and severity of state repression'. *Journal of Conflict Resolution* 58 (1): 143–168.

Roy, Olivier. 2004. *Globalized Islam: The Search for a New Ummah*. New York: Columbia University Press.

Salem, Sara. 2020. *Anticolonial Afterlives in Egypt: The Politics of Hegemony*. Cambridge: Cambridge University Press.

Schmitter, Philippe. 2014. 'Reflections on "transitology": Before and after'. In *Reflections on Uneven Democracies: The Legacy of Guillermo O'Donnell*, by Daniel Brinks et al., Marcelo Leiras, and Scott Mainwaring, 71–86. Baltimore: Johns Hopkins University Press.

Sika, Nadine. 2019. 'Repression, cooptation and movement fragmentation: Evidence from the youth movement in Egypt'. *Political Studies* 67 (3): 676–692.

Sika, Nadine. 2020. 'Contentious activism and political trust in non-democratic regimes: Evidence from the MENA'. *Democratization* 27 (8): 1515–1532.

Sika, Nadine. 2023. 'Mobilization, repression and policy concessions in authoritarian regimes: The cases of Egypt and Jordan'. *Political Studies*, 0 (0). https://doi.org/10.1177/00323217221141426

Skocpol, Theda. 1994. *States and Social Revolutions: A Comparative Analysis of France, Russia and China*. Cambridge: Cambridge University Press.

Stolleis, Friederike. 2018. 'Civic engagement'. In *Coping with Uncertainty: Youth in the Middle East and North Africa*, by Jörg Gertel and Ralph Hexel, 279–297. London: Saqi.

Teti, Andrea, Pamela Abbott, Valeria Talbot, and Paolo Maggiolini. 2020. *Democratization against Democracy: How EU Foreign Policy Fails in the Middle East*. Cham, Switzerland: Palgrave Macmillan.

Tilly, Chalres. 1993. *European Revolutions, 1492–1992*. Oxford: Blackwell.

Trantidis, Aris. 2021. 'Building an authoritarian regime: Strategies for autocratization and resistance in Belarus and Slovakia'. *The British Journal of Politics and International Relations* 24 (1) DOI: 10.1177/1369148120978964.

Tripp, Charles. 2013. *The Power and the People: Paths of Resistance in the Middle East*. Cambridge: Cambridge University Press.

Truex, Roru. 2019. 'Focal points, dissident calendars, and preemptive repression'. *Journal of Conflict Resolution* 63 (4): 1032–1052.

Van Til, Jon. 2015. 'Democratic resurgence in Hungary: Challenges to oppositional movements (an open-ended conclusion)'. In *The Hungarian Patient. Social Opposition to an Illiberal Democracy* by P. Krasztev and J. van Til, 367–384. Budapest-New York: CEU Press.

Vogel, Sasha de. 2022. 'Anti-opposition crackdowns and protest: The case of Belarus, 2000–2019'. *Post-Soviet Affairs* 38 (1–2): 9–25.

Way, Lucan. 2015. *Pluralism by Default: Weak Autocrats and the Rise of Competitive Politics*. Baltimore: Johns Hopkins University Press.

Wilson, Andrew. 2011. *Belarus: The Last European Dictatorship*. New Haven: Yale University Press.

Wintrobe, Ronald. 1998. *The Political Economy of Dictatorship*. Cambridge: Cambridge University Press.

Xu, Xu. 2021. 'To repress or to co-opt? Authoritarian control in the age of digital surveillance'. *American Journal of Political Science* 65 (2): 309–325.

Yom, Sean. 2016. From Resilience to Revolution: How Foreign Interventions Destabilize the Middle East. Columbia: Columbia University Press.

2
Widespread Repression and Political Threats against Civil Society in Egypt

Civil society has been an active and integral part of the Egyptian polity for decades, since before the 1952 coup d'état. After Gamal Abdel Nasser consolidated his power in June 1956, targeted repression against his political rivals and widespread repression against all civil society actors ensued. Nevertheless, by the 1990s, a decade into Mubarak's rule, civil society was flourishing, benefiting from the political and economic liberalization introduced by Mubarak (in power from 1981 to 2011), even though it was within the confines of considerable state control. Non-governmental organizations (NGOs), charitable and women's rights organizations, independent syndicates and unions, and human rights organizations started to flourish.

Not long after Mubarak's ouster, the interim regime—the supreme council for the armed forces (SCAF) headed by Field Marshal Tantawi—increased its repression against civil society actors. This crackdown seemed to be targeted initially at international democracy promotion foundations and human rights organizations, or at any organization receiving funding from these foundations. Nevertheless, in the period after the 2013 coup d'état against Morsi, which was followed by an autocratization and authoritarian regime-building process, repression became rampant against all civil society actors, whether they were charitable bodies, human rights organizations, Islamist or secular movements, syndicates or unions. Why did the new regime increase its repressive strategies against all civil society actors after the 25 January uprising that toppled Mubarak? What was the context in which political threats developed to constrain civil society's ability to network and develop coalitions that could advance socioeconomic and political change?

As argued in the 'Introduction' and in Chapter 1, it is largely assumed in the literature that authoritarian regimes make a distinction between different civil society actors, and those that are pro-charity and pro-development are mostly tolerated, while those associated with political opposition are repressed (Cheskin and March 2015). The literature also assumes that authoritarian regimes tend to use targeted repression against their opponents to limit violence and to avert public mobilization. This chapter challenges both these assertions through a nuanced analysis of the political context after the breakdown of the authoritarian Mubarak regime in 2011. It demonstrates that a recent historical experience of authoritarian regime breakdown impacts a newly established regime's perception of threat from civil society actors. It also impacts the autocratization process, whereby widespread repression is utilized against all civil society actors to demobilize and disempower the public. The consequences of widespread repression against civil society actors are analysed through semi-structured interviews and focus groups with civil society actors in Egypt. This chapter looks at three main contentious events that have shaped the regime's perception of threat from civil society, and which have also shaped the regime's utilization of coercion and widespread repression against these actors.

In social movement studies, there are certain transformative events that are public and visible, and that become part of the cultural development of a movement and how a regime acts and reacts to the movement (Hess and Martin 2006). This chapter first demonstrates how historically different regimes have utilized repression and cooptation towards civil society. It shows how the Naser regime used excessive violence and curtailed the work of civil society in the 1950s and 1960s. This is in contrast to the Mubarak regime, whose main strategy was to coopt and use targeted repression against certain civil society actors, mainly those in the political opposition. Then, the chapter shows that in the post-Mubarak Egypt, three major contentious events have shaped the Egyptian regime's strategies towards civil society actors and fuelled to the rise of widespread repression: (1) the 25 January uprising; (2) the mobilization of 30 June 2013, and the ensuing Raba'a Square massacre; and (3) the mobilization for the 'land'—the Tiran and Sanafir demonstration. In this chapter I discuss the first two events and how these have influenced how the regime has been utilizing repression in the public sphere. I also look at how the regime's repressive policies have shaped and impacted civil society's functions and ability to work in the polity. In Chapter 3 I discuss the second two events and their effect on the 'political' opposition, protest movements, and independent activists.

Brief Historical Context from Nasser to Mubarak

In 1952, the Egyptian officer corps led a coup d'état against then King Farouk in an effort to decolonize Egypt and end the British occupation. The few years preceding the coup d'état, especially following Egypt's involvement in the 1948 war in Palestine, were marked with heightened street contention against the ruling elites. A major contentious event was on 25 January 1952, when the government deployed the police force to resist British troops' occupation of Ismailia, which resulted in the death and injury of a large number of police officers. Demonstrations erupted directly afterwards, and buildings in downtown Cairo were set on fire, yet when asked to intervene to stop contention, the military did not abide by these orders, marking a major rift between the monarchical regime and the military apparatus. A few months later, the coup took place. The aim of the army was initially to liberate the country from British occupation and to develop a reform-oriented civilian government, while restoring the military's capability to defend the nation. Nevertheless, immediately after the coup, the army was split between those who wanted to return to the barracks and install democracy, and those who wanted to directly rule the nation. The first camp was led by Mohamed Naguib, who was appointed as the first president after the coup, while the second camp was led by Nasser and sought to establish a 'military regime to revolutionize society from above' (Kandil 2012, 16). The power struggle between the two camps ended with the removal of Naguib, which prompted popular mobilization in favour of Naguib.[1]

Once the power struggle ended with Nasser securing his hold on power, targeted and widespread repressive strategies emerged. Targeted repression was utilized against the security forces, the military camp that was associated with Naguib, and the political elite who had dominated power during the monarchical era. Meanwhile, widespread repression was utilized against the public, mainly through arbitrary arrests and detentions of demonstrators who mobilized on the streets in support of Naguib. Nasser then embarked on establishing a strong security force that was dependent on the military and the security apparatus to replace the previous power centres in the polity. By the early 1960s, repression was widespread, with over 20,000 political prisoners and detainees filling the country's prisons. Surveillance was at an apogee; phones, homes, offices, and citizens' daily lives were controlled. The Ministry of Interior and the intelligence organs associated with it had increasing power and used coercion against any dissent, or potential dissent. The Nasser regime relied 'to a large extent on fear as a preemptive device to contain threats, and exercising outright coercion' (Ryan 2001, 33). The Islamists, the Brotherhood in particular, were targeted by the regime. Arbitrary arrests and detentions were pervasive during the Nasserist state development process. While arrests and detentions were increasing in number and scope, new laws

---

[1] For more discussions on this contentious event see chapter 2 in Sika, Nadine. 2023. *Youth in Egypt: Identity, Participation and Opportunity*. New York: New York University Press.

to hamper civil society actors and to control the media were promulgated, as will be shown in the following section (Kienle 2021).

After Nasser's sudden death in 1970, Anwar El-Sadat, a member of the Free Officers Movement and vice-president at the time, took power. Upon taking power, the use of repression and coercion against civil society changed. Sadat promised not to use excessive repression against citizens, while purging Nasser's leadership of the intelligence services and embarking on demilitarizing the polity. He retained the coercive institutions; however, he granted more power to the police and interior ministry than the military. Arbitrary arrests and detentions were not used except under threatening circumstances, like the 1977 bread riots and the 1980–1981 crackdown on opposition and intellectuals. These were characterized by more targeted repressive strategies, however, rather than widespread and diffuse repression (Ryan 2001).

After Sadat's assassination and Mubarak's ascendence to power in 1981, 'repression under the Mubarak regime was not as wholesale or indiscriminate as that of its predecessors' (Ryan 2001, 35). Yet targeted repression, especially towards the Brotherhood, was pervasive (Nugent 2020).

Dominating and Hegemonizing Civil Society

Prior to the 2011 uprising, Egyptian civil society had experienced three stages of development. From the nineteenth century until World War II, the major actors were philanthropic organizations in close contact with the then royal family. In 1945, the first law circumscribing civil society—the Charities and Social Institutions Code—was implemented. This facilitated coordination among various organizations, which were increasing in number and scope (Agati 2007). The second stage was during Nasser's tenure, from 1954 until the 1970s. During the early years of his rule, full control was imposed over social institutions. The social pact at the time was clear: 'As long as the state was developing economically and providing for its citizens in a basic way, citizens did not demand democracy' (Agati 2007, 58). No political parties were allowed to exist apart from the Arab Socialist Union (ASU), which was closely tied to the regime. Independent civil society organizations were also restricted. In 1964, the Civic Association Code, Law 32 of 1964, was promulgated. This gave the Nasser regime the right to reject the establishment of any organization that it deemed to be against its interests (Agati 2007). The Emergency Law, Law 162 of 1958, came into force in 1967, during the Arab-Israeli war. Until 2021, except for a few months in the 1980s, Egypt was subject to the Emergency Law.

[This law] has been continuously extended every three years since 1981. Under the law, police powers are expanded, constitutional rights suspended, and censorship legalized. The law sharply circumscribes any non-governmental political activity: street demonstrations, non-approved political organizations, and unregistered financial donations are formally banned.

(Agati 2007, 58)

These strategies, which were first installed by the Nasser regime, demonstrate the extent to which newly established authoritarian regimes tend to autocratize their regimes through reliance on widespread repression against civil society actors and citizens at large. These strategies vary from physical repression to the development of coercive institutions. Additionally, these regimes control all social institutions through laws that hamper independent work.

Mubarak, Targeted Repression, and the Co-Optation of Civil Society

By the 1980s, under Hosni Mubarak's regime (1981–2011), a new space for civil society actors had emerged on the understanding that they were becoming an important force for helping the government's development efforts (Sika 2018; Agati 2007). In 2002, Law 84 on NGOs replaced Law 84 of 1964. It still controlled the work of civil society actors but was less restrictive than the 1964 law. The new law also controlled foreign funding, especially that channelled to human rights organizations. During this stage, Mubarak developed a corporate strategy whereby he encouraged the establishment of civil society organizations, most importantly NGOs, while simultaneously coopting them into the state's development scheme.

He ensured that they would not pose a political threat to his power by placing individuals and entrepreneurs in charge of them who were closely associated with him and his family. Many of the directors of the boards of civil society organizations were parliamentarians and/or government officials. Civil society actors, however, believed that in order to survive, they had to cooperate with the bureaucracy and state security apparatus, as well as with the various networks of privilege in the polity (Sika 2023; Agati 2016). In this respect, civil society was not separate from politics but became an inseparable part of it (Gervasio and Teti 2020).

Opposition political parties and NGOs have been tolerated by the regime as long as they did not cross certain red lines. Since the late 1950s, Egypt has had a non-competitive political system, moving from a single party, the Arab Socialist Union, to a dominant political party, the National Democratic Party. The former was established by Nasser, and the latter by Sadat. In the 1980s, open electoral systems were introduced for opposition political parties, and the 1990s saw a plethora of NGOs and civil society organizations established (Albrecht 2005). Various national councils were set up to coopt civil society actors, most importantly the National Council for Human Rights, established in 2003 as a committee to consult with government bodies on human rights matters.

> In three ministries (Interior, Justice and Foreign Affairs), offices have been established to deal with human rights issues and keep up the dialogue with the respective NGOs. Those also communicate constantly with the state security forces (*amn ad-dawla*), which set the limits for the NGOs' engagement. Areas that are out of bounds for debate include the president of the republic and his family, the military, national unity and minority affairs (Copts), relations with Saudi Arabia, and some religious issues.
>
> **(Albrecht 2005, 385)**

Civil society actors were able to register as institutions or business enterprises in order to function more freely and avoid being subjected to government intervention. Some, especially human rights organizations, registered themselves as companies, while others did not register at all. Law 84 for the year 2002 encouraged charitable and social organizations (CSOs) to work in other areas, rather than political activities. Hence, many actors blended civil society work with political work. 'In the absence of other platforms of political expression, CSOs became venues for political contestation between different groups that were hitherto excluded from power and were unable to mobilize mass support around their political programs' (Brown et al. 2021, 96–97). Within the realm of the hegemonized public sphere under Mubarak, some activists were, however, able to become independent and be 'partly' organic intellectuals (Gervasio and Teti 2020, 1099).[2]

Restrictions on protest movements and independent student movements were extreme. Political gatherings and public demonstrations were few, and the security services maintained a tight grip on a number of activists. The security apparatus was powerful and 'omnipresent, and rarely were protests allowed to freely assemble or move' (Stacher 2020, 102). Nevertheless, neither the security forces nor the military used force or opened fire against protesters

---

[2] For more discussion on the Gramscian perspective on civil society in the Middle East, please refer to Chapter 1.

on the streets since their demonstrations of force in 1986, when Mubarak called on the army to end riots by the conscripts (Stacher 2020).

The 25 January Uprising

Activism and contentious politics were vigorous in the decade preceding Mubarak's ouster. Many new movements had been established, such as Kifaya, the Youth for Change movement, the April 6 youth movement, 'We Are All Khalid Said', and the Revolutionary Socialists.[3] The weeks leading up to Mubarak's ouster demonstrated the ability of these movements to mobilize large numbers of individuals on the streets, not only in Cairo but in other governorates as well, most importantly Suez. When the police encountered the first wave of demonstrations on 25 January 2011, they used repression and tear gas to stop the mobilization. Nevertheless, young activists mobilized further and were able to restart their mobilization and demonstrations a few days later on what is known as the 'Friday of Anger', which led to an eighteen-day uprising demanding Mubarak's ouster before they would leave Tahrir Square (Shehata 2011; Aoudé 2013; Chalcraft 2012; Sika 2023).[4] On 11 February, Mubarak stepped down and the military took power in the interim. The mere fact that civil society actors, and young activists in particular, were able to mobilize a large number of citizens onto the streets made a strong impression on the ruling elite in the months and years to come. One response was clear: to demobilize the public.

The Conflict–Dissent Nexus

The literature on conflict and dissent has identified three main reasons for repressive tactics. First, autocratic regimes are responsive to protests, modifying their behaviour to some extent, and they resort to repression only when all else fails. Second, repression can work as a deterrent to political mobilization, when the regime raises the costs of protest. Third, repression is a function of a regime's calculations regarding the costs and benefits of the use of force and of activists' ability to mobilize. Repression is therefore applied when the

---

[3] For more discussion on these movements see, for instance, Nadine Sika, *Youth Activism*; Maha Abdel Rahman, *Egypt's Long Revolution*.

[4] Mubarak's ouster itself is highly contested by scholars. Some believe that without the military's intervention he would not have stepped down, others that the mass mobilization was the main reason for his ouster (see, for example, Sean McMahon 2013; Hazem Kandil 2012, 2016; Maha Abdel Rahman 2015). I believe it is a combination of both, whereby the military would not have intervened or would not have ousted him had the mass demonstrations not taken place.

regime perceives that it could be advantageous in maintaining or extending social and political control, or when a protest is not influencing the rest of society. This is assessed based on the size of the protest, the protesters' willingness to use violence, and the media coverage (Chen 2018; Göbel 2021). However, regime-led repression is risky because it can prompt even more demonstrations (Göbel 2021) as an unintended consequence, if a large number of people perceive the regime's use of force to be illegitimate (Opp and Roehl 1990; Grimm and Harders 2018).

The responses to repression help to understand how it impacts demobilization in authoritarian regimes. Here, a distinction should be made between the repressive strategies that are clearly enacted by the state and those that individuals perceive to be state repression, which is 'subjective' (Kurtzman 1996; Maher 2010; Honari 2018). Perceived repression negatively influences the belief in the efficacy of political participation and hence leads to demobilization. However, it can also increase grievances and stimulate further mobilization (Pearlman 2013; Honari 2018). In the case of Egypt, we see widespread repression applied across the board against all civil society actors in addition to targeted repression against the political opposition. In the following I shed light on the utilization of widespread repression against non-politicized civil society actors, while in Chapter 3 I shed light on how widespread repression is amalgamated with targeted repression towards the political opposition.

From the Fall of Mubarak to the Fall of Morsi: A New Beginning in Widespread Repression

The day after Mubarak's fall, the Supreme Council for the Armed Forces (SCAF) took power for an interim period. It was, however, unprepared to manage the political process and needed help from the only organized opposition—the Brotherhood (Stacher 2020). At the same time, SCAF began to engage in a subtle process of regime-led violence against any social force that was able to organize and mobilize people against the ruling elite. Their perception of threat from all civil society actors was high, because of the ability of civil society organizations to network and mobilize large numbers of citizens (Sika 2017). In the few weeks after Mubarak's ouster, the state-led media claimed that the uprising and subsequent unrest was the result of foreign-led interference against Egypt. They argued that a 'foreign agenda', a 'third agent', and mysterious 'hidden hands' were the main reasons why activists mobilized on the streets (Holmes 2019, 81). However, the foreign-led media used this same discourse, fuelling more suspicion, with many foreign media outlets suggesting that the Western democracy promotion foundations had helped young democrats in Egypt to force Mubarak from office. In addition, it was commented that 'the trainings that US-backed NGOs had offered to Egyptian activists had inspired their leadership of the mass peaceful protests' (Herrold 2020, 57). Hence, five months after SCAF took power, the first victims of regime-led repression were civil society actors, primarily those sponsored by Western democracy promotion programmes. The former minister of international cooperation, Fayza Abou El Naga held a speech to the Human Rights Committee of the Parliament, in February 2012, claiming that during the period from March 2011 until June of the same year, civil society organizations received USD 175 million in grants, whereas during the four years preceding the uprising, only USD 60 million were granted (Mogib 2013). These funds were given for democracy promotion in Egypt, however, the regime insinuated that these funds represented a threat to the Egyptian state. The Ministry of Justice started to investigate all the activities and funding sources of different NGOs, including those that received support from the European Union and the US.

> Thirty-nine Egyptian and foreign organizations were operating while unregistered, twenty-eight Egyptian NGOs were receiving foreign funds illegally, and several foreign NGOs were participating in the types of political activities banned by law 84 of 2002. In early December, the Justice Ministry officially revealed that four hundred NGOs in Egypt had received foreign funding over the past six years and on December 24 al Masry al Youm released leaked data that NGOs 'and some famous Egyptian figures' received nearly 1.7 billion Egyptian pounds, or around $285 million in foreign funds since June 2010 alone.
>
> **(Herrold 2020, 65–66)**

Several NGO headquarters were raided in December, with the police seizing materials and arresting forty-three civil society workers on different charges, mostly for operating without a license, engaging in political activities, or receiving funds from international donors without permission Christensen and Weinstein 2013, 77). Soon, independent media and influential independent media figures were also targeted. In September a campaign against journalists began and some independent media outlets were raided by the police, allegedly for lack of proper licensing (Mansour 2015). In December, *Egypt Independent*—an independent media outlet—was shut down after publishing an article alleging divisions in the military.

The main movers of the mobilization against Mubarak then came under scrutiny, and the Ultras were targeted in early 2012.[5] Independent activists and demonstrators were also targeted during this time, especially whenever public demands and mobilization asked for substantial or radical change. The military's violence against demonstrators was systematic, coming almost once a month in the year following Mubarak's ouster (Kandil 2012). 'On February 1, 2012, during a match between Al-Ahly and Al-Masry teams in Port Said, fighting broke out that resulted in the death of 74 people, with over 1,000 injured. The doors to the stadium had been mysteriously locked, trapping people inside' (Holmes 2019, 76).

Development NGOs faced problems when the government blocked all approvals for foreign-funded development projects, even those benefiting employment, education, and health (Herrold 2020). Artists have also been the target of repressive measures. For instance, Ahmed Naji, a young novelist, was sentenced to two years in prison for violating 'public morality' by describing sex scenes and drug use in his novel (Stacher 2020). According to Stacher (2020, 98), 'we see an inverse relationship in which state violence rises as state capacity diminishes'. One of our informants, who used to work for an Egyptian NGO funded by an American funding organization, explained:

> My previous organization was registered with the Ministry of Social Solidarity, yet I was detained three times. We go to subaltern areas with all the legal documentation, the police come in and take us to the police station to inquire why we are here and what we are doing. When they see that we have the necessary permissions, we are still told to go to the police station prior to our interaction with the people on the ground.[6]

Another worker at a development NGO said that:

> There is always mistrust from the government's side toward us ... for them, civil society organizations are always associated with foreigners, and with receiving hard currency in US dollars, thus we work as agents ... I'm always afraid because any time I could be threatened by the security personnel and the security is always

---

[5] For more discussion on the Ultras and their role in pre- and post-Mubarak Egypt, see Nadine Sika, *Youth Activism and Contentious Politics in Egypt*; see also Connor T. Jerzak, 2013 'Ultras in Egypt: State, revolution, and the power of public space'. *Interface: A Journal for and about Social Movements* 5 (2): 240–262; and Robert Wolterin, 2013 'Unusual suspects: "Ultras" as political actors in the Egyptian revolution'. *Arab Studies Quarterly* 36 (3): 290–304.

[6] Interview, August 2018.

at my back. My work is very precarious, and sometimes after I finish meetings with government officials, I break down and cry because I do not understand why they do this.[7]

NGOs associated with some of the foreign foundations that were questioned in November 2011 have had to shut down, either for a few months or permanently. For instance, one organization that had been working on peace closed down in 2011 for a few months. According to one of its founding members: 'We closed because some of our personnel started to have some security problems; the security would call them to go to the police station and be randomly questioned. So we decided to shut down for a while in 2011, because the social and political environments were not right at the moment'.[8] But in 2013 the organization closed down indefinitely.

Even though violence erupted against civil society actors in the few months after Mubarak's ouster, the scope and breadth of repression was still limited until mid-2013. The repression mainly targeted foreign-funded NGOs, while other self-funded organizations, campaigns, initiatives, movements, and even political parties were allowed to function. Between 2011 and 2013, civil and political engagement increased enormously and dialogue between civil society actors and the regime took place. During this time, however, a 'balance of weakness' was established. The enforcement arm of the Mubarak regime, especially the police force and security apparatus, had been temporarily defeated, although they remained contenders during this time (Kandil 2012, 241), while the weakness of the political opposition and civil society actors was exposed.

The 30 June 'Revolution'

The first two years after Mubarak's fall were characterized by political uncertainty, alliance building, and alliance breaking between the secular opposition and the Muslim Brotherhood. Once the military started to gain ground in the political and public spheres and the Brotherhood was no longer seen as useful, the military decided to hegemonize the polity. Establishing a new political order became the objective. To do so, in any country, state violence is utilized to get rid of the old political and social forces. The new regime is built through destroying the previous order, along with its political and economic elite (Stacher 2020, 108). During Morsi's short tenure,

---

[7] Interview, June 2018.
[8] Interview, October 2018.

he and the Brotherhood colluded with the military. They were helping and developing alliances with the military and the Ministry of Interior, to the detriment of opposition activists (Grimm 2022). When Morsi made a constitutional declaration granting himself and the military more powers, opposition against him increased, old political opposition networks were re-established through the National Salvation Front (NSF), and demonstrations, strikes, and contestations against him intensified. But the police disobeyed Morsi's demand to move against the mobilized public (Grimm 2022, 77). Many protest events and a few months later, activists developed a campaign called Tamarrod, mobilizing the collection of signatures for Morsi's resignation, and to revoke the 2012 constitution and return temporarily to the 1971 constitution until a new one could be written. The campaign started as a network of former opposition activists from the Kifaya and April 6 movements. However, within a few weeks it received financial and logistical support from the state security apparatus (Ketchley 2017; Springborg 2018; Grimm 2022). Clashes increased between the supporters and opponents of Tamarrod, which called for demonstrations on 30 June 2013, the anniversary of Morsi's first year in office. In response, the Brotherhood and their affiliates called for demonstrations in Raba'a al-Adawiyya Mosque and al-Nahda Square (Grimm 2022).

At this stage, a rupture between the old and new regimes became evident. The thrust now was not to reinstate the older status quo, but to construct a new regime based on military power, with the military and its security apparatus at the centre of political power. An escalation in violence followed, aimed at ridding the regime not only of the old ruling elite, but also of the old opposition and the civil society organizations that had existed for the previous three decades. '[T]he state violence everywhere witnessed after the post-uprising turmoil is not about containing a failing order, but creating a new one' (Stacher 2020, 99).

> Ousting Morsi was easy. Demobilizing millions of Egyptians was much more difficult and much more bloody. This was because the coup emerged from within society—and thus it was the society that had the potential to threaten Sisi … the period leading up to July 3 was characterized by large-scale street protests. They increased after July 3 when supporters of the Brotherhood staged protests. Although these protests were smaller in size, they still were seen as a threat to the regime. Dealing with the continuation of street protests—both Islamists and secular opposition, was a much more difficult task than removing the president.
>
> **(Holmes 2019, 151)**

Repression and Fear as Tools against Mobilization and Dissent

Fear has an obvious negative effect on dissent by heightening risk aversion and pessimism (Young 2019; Li and Elfstrom 2021). Most research on this issue analyses the effect of fear on mobilization/demobilization in repressive regimes. However, it does not look at how fear also encourages demobilization and puts pressure on all civil society actors, not only on protesters and/or dissidents.[9] The fieldwork with civil society actors in Egypt demonstrates that fear, propagated through an authoritarian regime's strategies of widespread repression against charity workers and civically engaged individuals, undermines their ability to work, network, or lead the socioeconomic and cultural change to which they aspire.

With Morsi, the elimination of the Brotherhood and the secular opposition, the regime-building process advanced to repress and hegemonize the public sphere at the same time. Law 84 of 2002 governing NGOs remained the main instrument for controlling them until 2014, when Sisi amended Article 78 of the penal code. Any organization that was found to receive foreign funding, whether an NGO or not, might now be interpreted by the regime as a threat to the national interest, unity, public peace, or Egyptian national security, and its leaders could face penalties of life in prison or large fines of Egyptian Pounds (LE) 500,000[10] and more (Herrold 2020). This was a direct threat to the human rights organizations and to all other civil society actors, since many of these organizations were not registered under the NGO law. Once this amendment became part of the penal code, an organization's legal status no longer mattered. After a few months, the regime published a statement in the government-owned newspaper *al-Ahram* to the effect that all organizations working as civic associations had to register within forty-five days, and those that did not comply would face prosecution and security investigation. Following this up, the police started raiding different organizations and issuing travel bans against a large number of civil society organization employees, in addition to freezing their assets. The majority of human rights organizations working in Egypt at that time were included in these measures. Directors and activists, mostly from high-profile

---

[9] Some scholars argue that repression is utilized not only to demobilize but also to build consent among the population, but this is beyond the scope of this book. See, for instance, Jean Lachapelle, 2022. 'Repression reconsidered: Bystander effects and legitimation in authoritarian regimes'. *Comparative Politics*. Online first doi: 10.5129/001041522X16317396828722

[10] This was almost USD32,000 in 2022.

human rights organizations, had their assets frozen and were banned from travel (Herrold 2020).

In 2017, Law 84 was promulgated, legalizing threats and constraints against the establishment, funding, operation, and most importantly the autonomy of civil society organizations.[11] A large number of charitable organizations, estimated by some as almost a thousand, had been forcibly shut down by the regime in 2014 as allegedly affiliated with the Brotherhood. Other non-religious organizations were also forcibly shut down, and state-led propaganda increased against the Brotherhood. However, the majority of functioning civil society organizations, especially NGOs, shut down, froze their work, or developed social entrepreneurship and start-ups to reposition themselves away from regime scrutiny. In our sample, forty-seven individuals said that their major problem today is regime repression; sixteen said it was state propaganda in the media against civil society actors; and eighteen said that it was the undermining of the groups by security forces' tactics like cooptation and divide and rule. Twenty-nine individuals stated that they have disengaged from both civic and political engagement as a result of the rising repression against their organizations.

In 2019, a week before President Sisi's meeting with Donald Trump (Al-Monitor 2019), the minister of social solidarity announced a new law regulating the work of civil associations, Law 149, which would control NGOs. This law is believed to be as restrictive as the 2017 law, but with more curbs on research and public opinion surveys. The text loosely defines national security, public order, and public morals, and extends the regime's powers to restrict and monitor civil society actors (Human Rights Watch 2019).

The majority of civil society actors in our sample (seventy-one out of 111) argued that this NGO law, in addition to the terrorist entity law had a negative effect on them. Nine interviewees explained that their organizations had shut down completely as a result of this law. One member of a charitable organization argued that: 'The NGO law[12] is a security issue par excellence … some security provisions were not present in previous laws but now the law stipulates that the *mukhabarat* [intelligence] have to grant permission for our activities'.[13] Another argued that:

---

[11] For more details on this law and its different provisions see Catherine Herrold, 2020. *Delta Democracy: Pathways to Incremental Civic Revolution in Egypt and Beyond*. New York: Oxford University Press.

[12] The fieldwork was conducted during the summer and fall of 2018, and hence all reference to the NGO law is to Law 84 of 2017.

[13] Interview, June 2018.

> During the past year we have been having trouble working, our work has almost stalled. There are a few projects we were working on where we need the Ministry of Social Solidarity's permission, but we were not able to [receive it] because of the new law. This law does not even have regulations, so we do not know what is permissible and what is not ... so now we are just waiting. A major hurdle is receiving the permissions for work. For instance, if you want to start a project in three months, it goes for security permissions for six to nine months, and with the bureaucracy, we actually receive the permission after 11 months. This means that we cannot work and reach out to our constituents. This is very frustrating, and it halts our projects.[14]
>
> Since the adoption of the new NGO law, we live under threat. A large number of our activities have stalled, as all of a sudden, we have become an illegal organization ... we did not shut down but we are working in the shadows. If anyone knows that we are still working then I will be jailed. Now we do not host any activities. We are afraid that any of the participants in our events could be an informer and we will get into trouble. The problem today is that we do not know the red lines. Previously we knew that we were fine as long as we did not mobilize people for demonstrations or talk politics.[15]

It was very evident that the space once available for social and cultural work was no longer tolerated.

> The general environment in the world and in Egypt is not promoting our work. The new law constrains a lot of our work ... the space we have is shrinking all the time ... you cannot imagine ... before we do any step, we have to take permissions. To organize a workshop or a conference we have to have permission. If we will do fieldwork with stakeholders or survey questionnaires, we have to send our questionnaire to the security.[16]

Many organizations had provided a space in which others could interact, maintain dialogue, and debate the different socioeconomic and political issues that became popular in the late 2000s. A member of one such organization says that: 'By 2015 we shut down, because we have seen that the security has gone to similar spaces like ours and confiscated everything; they also went to different apartments in downtown to see what people are doing. In early 2015 we closed for a while, because our neighbors told us that security came and asked about us'.[17]

---

[14] Interview, August 2018.
[15] Interview, June 2018.
[16] Interview, June 2018.
[17] Interview, June 2018.

Civil society actors who focus only on charitable or development issues are also afraid that at any time the security could come and shut their organizations down. An interviewee working in an organization to combat violence against women is aware that her work is very risky, because under the new law, the government has the authority to close down her organization at any time.[18] The dilemma of foreign funding is putting pressure on civil society actors and halting much of their work. Some civil society actors working on peace building and dialogue have argued that they are under too much pressure to work and receive funds from or cooperate with donors, even the United Nations (UN). 'In the current environment in Egypt, no one is able to receive funds from abroad, because you will be in the spotlight'.[19] Organizations working on cultural and social issues prefer to receive funds from Egyptian foundations like Misr El Kheir, a Cairo-based non-profit development institution, or from Egyptian corporations. For instance, an organization working on the relationship between peace and charity wanted to cooperate with the UN for the international day for charity, but the Ministry of Interior denied them permission.[20]

An interviewee working on development issues in general, and on women's empowerment issues in particular, maintains that they are able to survive the regime crackdown and are not shutting down; however, they receive many threats from the security apparatus. 'Previously our organization was able to develop projects independently from start to end. However, now we are not able to; we only conduct workshops for our stakeholders'.[21]

Some actors in NGOs were forced to leave their positions due to a lack of funding opportunities, and as a result, projects could not be implemented. An interviewee who worked in monitoring and evaluation (M&E) at a local NGO for women's empowerment said that:

> I changed my career because previously I was working on certain projects, and when they were done, we were unable to receive and sustain previous funding. This was a result of the fact that this NGO was unable to receive the security permissions to start new projects, so I had to go. The main problem was security clearance. The Ministry of Social Solidarity did not have a problem with [us] being funded for women's empowerment purposes. However, they did not receive the security clearance and hence we were unable to work … Some of these projects were on

---

[18] Interview, July 2018.
[19] Interview, June 2018.
[20] Interview, May 2018.
[21] Interview, August 2018.

women's empowerment, mainly educating young women to participate in their local elections.[22]

Certain governorates and cities can no longer be visited by civil society organizations. One person working in an international NGO said that:

> The security said that now we are not allowed to work in Aswan, Matruh New Wadi, North/South Sinai, Port Said, Ismailia and Suez … [although] it's not officially on paper. I'm saying this from a point where I and my organization have very good relations with security on both the personal and professional levels … so this is putting us under a lot of pressure, because one of our missions is to bring in people from all governorates who do not have economic and employment opportunities and to help them find different opportunities through workshops and material incentives.[23]

Some organization members contend that they have not received any permissions to work with their stakeholders since 2015.

> At first they [the security] alleged that anything that has to do with political participation for women will not be permitted. After Raba'a, the security started to increase, and the internal splits among civil society actors and human rights organizations in particular increased. This was an important factor for the security apparatus, and they used it to their advantage to further fragment any remaining networks among civil society activists. Some saw this as slaughter, while others saw it as justified, citing that it was in accordance with international law … some went to the extreme right, others to the extreme left, so the security apparatus prevailed.
>
> In 2014 we utilized an opportunity which happens only every four years, namely the discussion on the status of human rights in Egypt. Our bad luck, however, was that it was in November 2014, after Raba'a … so we had to say and discuss all human rights abuses that occurred during this incidence. After the report was out, there were 92 or 93 recommendations … even though the report was not particularly on Raba'a, it was on violence against women, yet we were still questioned by the security apparatus and were in a lot of trouble. Another organization that worked with us on this report, XX was banned, and since then we have been under pressure and security surveillance.[24]

---

[22] Interview, August 2018.
[23] Interview, August 2018.
[24] Interview, June 2018.

Widespread Repression and Political Threats against Civil Society in Egypt 61

Civil society actors working in the field of culture and the arts are also targeted. A hip-hop artist who had a few songs on YouTube that were very successful in 2010 argued that:

> One of the main problems of the poorness of content today is because we cannot talk about politics … We had made a short film earlier, but I cannot talk about this issue now.[25] Today we are used to publishing work on YouTube and in the span of two hours the content is removed, even if it has nothing to do with politics. For instance, two hours after I published some content the other month … I received a phone call from someone I do not know who instructed me to delete the video … I am not allowed to work with XX because he is a member of April 6; I also cannot work with XXX or XX because they are in exile. There are certain black-listed stars that are not allowed even on YouTube.[26]

Another informant working on youth empowerment through art said that they practice self-censorship and censorship of the young people who display their art with the NGO:

> Sometimes they [young artists] draw things that I think might put them in trouble so I do not put it on display … For instance, in our organization, we do not talk about religion, politics or sex [the biggest red lines], so when young people discuss anything, especially on stage, about their own opinions, I myself get very scared. I am scared for security reasons, so when they talk about political issues in a play, for instance, and any public figure is present, it becomes very scary. For instance, one of our young people was on stage and he cited Ahmed Foad Negm's[27] poem, which is very political … I was really afraid, but luckily nothing happened.[28]

Similarly, a member of a choir group, said that: 'I'm part of a choir group, but we were told that we are not allowed to go and sing at the Tali'a [Vanguard] Theatre[29] because if you do you can make a revolutionary moment …

---

[25] This interview was conducted in a café and the interviewee did not want to discuss personal and political matters in case someone informed the police of the conversation and/or interview.
[26] Interview, July 2018.
[27] Ahmed Foad Negm was a famous Egyptian poet who wrote revolutionary poems in colloquial Arabic. For more information on his life and death, see https://blogs.transparent.com/arabic/ahmed-fouad-negm/.
[28] Interview, July 2018.
[29] This public-owned theatre was established by Nasser, along with several other theatres, in the 1960s. For more information on this and other public theatres see, for instance, https://akhbarak.net/news/15003221/articles/30264297/%D9%85%D9%86%D8%B7%D9%82%D8%AA%D9%8A-%D8%AF%D9%84%D9%8A%D9%84%D9%83-%D9%84%D8%AA%D8%A7%D8%B1%D9%8A%D8%AE-%D9%85%D8%B3%D8%A7%D8%B1%D8%AD-%D8%A7%D9%84%D8%A8%D9%8A%D8%AA-%D8%A7%D9%84%D9%81%D9%86%D9%8A-%D9%84%D9%84%D9%85%D8%B3%D8%B1%D8%AD-%D9%81%D9%8A#:~:text=%D9%8A%D8%B9%D9%88%D8%AF%20%D8%AA

for instance, during one theatre program at El Seid club, all the artists were rounded up by the police'.[30]

Controlling CSOs through GONGOs

The concept that civil society might be independent and express alternative views is contrary to the regime's perceptions and ideas, and the regime is moving towards repositioning all NGOs as government-led organizations, or GONGOs (Holmes 2019). The attempt to shut down all independent outlets and make them dependent on the regime illustrates its coercive strategies and determination to enforce hegemony. The first step in this direction was the establishment of the Tahya Misr fund in 2014, when President Sisi launched the donation process by donating half his salary to the fund. The regime then put pressure on all large businesses to donate to this fund.[31] Later, this fund would give NGOs money to work on their own development initiatives. Fifty-one per cent of our respondents—almost half—argued that they have to work closely with the government in order to accomplish their work. By demonstrating the importance of these official partnerships for the work of civil society organizations, it is clear that the regime is intent on dominating civil society to ensure that it can influence whatever activities take place in the public sphere and direct civil society actors towards its own mainstream development objectives. Identifying the leading actors in civil society and controlling them and their work is a key strategy. A member of an organization working on social and cultural development contends that:

> It is difficult to work on your own; when we say that we are an independent NGO and want to do some research, we are not allowed to do so by the regime. Today there is some kind of 'nationalization' [ta'meem] of projects. To be able to do anything you need to have a partnership with the government ... you are not able to work or receive funds for any large project if you do not cooperate with the government ... it is either you work with them or you do not exist. Even international donors do not fund you if you do not work with the government, because if you do not do so, you will not be granted permissions to work.[32]

D8%A7%D8%B1%D9%8A%D8%AE%20%D9%85%D8%B3%D8%B1%D8%AD%20%D8%A7%D9%84%D8%B7%D9%84%D9%8A%D8%B9%D8%A9%20(%D9%85%D8%B3%D8%B1%D8%AD,%D8%A8%D8%A7%D9%84%D8%B3%D9%8A%D8%AF%D8%A9%20%D8%B2%D9%8A%D9%86%D8%A8%20%D8%A3%D9%88%20%D9%82%D8%A7%D8%B9%D8%A9%20%D8%A5%D9%8A%D9%88%D8%A7%D8%B1%D8%AA.

[30] Interview, Cairo, July 2018.
[31] For more information on this fund see https://tahyamisrfund.org.
[32] Interview, July 2018.

Similarly, an interviewee working in an NGO that partners with the National Council for Women explains:

> I believe that without working with the government we will not accomplish anything. There are people who we cannot reach out to without the contacts we receive from the government ... we have contacts with the Ministry of Youth and Ministry of Education in addition to protocols with different public schools ... Even though we face many problems over security permissions, compared to others it seems that we do not face problems ... [but] before going in the field or doing research, we need security permissions. Yet we still receive a lot of phone calls from the security apparatus about our fieldwork. We answer all their questions, but we are always threatened.[33]

Others have argued that working on education or with children in public schools is not possible unless you receive permissions from the Ministry of Education to work on the ground.

Nevertheless, with the increased dominance of the security apparatus in the public sphere, sometimes working with the government is not sufficient. In some instances, the ministries accept certain projects, which are then not granted permission by the security apparatus. 'A lot of things do not get security clearance and hence they do not receive permissions. We are not allowed to contest this ... sometimes you look at projects and you do not understand how they [the security] approved it, and at others, you do not understand why they did not ... there is no manual.'[34]

Another interviewee said that:

> To work on youth empowerment issues, we had to be in contact with the Ministry of Youth and Sport, because they facilitate the spaces for our workshops. At some centers we have to provide [both] the security and the ministry with the content of the workshop, what the questions/answers and discussions are, but at others we do not. It depends on where the centers are located. My work cannot function without the help of the government because it is the only one that has the space for me to work and reach out to youth. So when the ministry is cooperative it facilitates a lot of things, especially security permissions.[35]

In its attempt to demobilize the public, the regime increased its coercive measures, but also used other means to hegemonize the public sphere. During

---

[33] Interview, August 2018.
[34] Interview, July 2018.
[35] Interview, August 2018.

interviews with government officials, I was told by two bureaucrats at the Ministry of Social Solidarity and another at the Ministry of Education that the government is now keen to work only with large civil society organizations, in particular Tahya Masr and Misr El Kheir, since these are the most 'reliable' NGOs in the public sphere. They know what the government's vision is for development and they pursue it.[36]

Building Government–Civil Society Partnerships

In our sample, seventy-one interviewees said that they also cooperate with other civil society organizations working in similar fields. Two organizations we contacted described their primary mission as empowering NGOs working in different fields. One of them, for instance, provided a 'space' to work and meet in for small NGOs that could not afford to buy their own offices. This organization used to have space for walk-ins to just sit down and discuss any individual civic project.[37] Cooperation mainly consists of creating public events together with other organizations, or hosting stakeholders from different organizations. 'Our headquarters is in Menoufiya governorate, so when we want to help our stakeholders with capacity building or help our own workers we send them to Cairo, to the main agency that we work with.'[38] There is also cooperation between different national NGOs: 'There are a lot of partnerships and networking between all NGOs working on education. In the end, no one is capable of doing anything alone, so cooperation has to happen between the NGOs working in one field, [and with] the donors and the government.'[39]

A number of cooperation measures and networks are, however, conducted through international organizations or UN agencies. Civil society actors have argued that to be able to cooperate with international funding organizations, 'we need to build cooperation with organizations working on similar issues to us.'[40] Some contend that when they want to cooperate with other organizations, they have to involve the relevant ministry. For instance, a member of an NGO working on public health said that their organization had agreed with another organization to build a hospital in a poor area, and that they would collect the needed funds through crowdfunding and personal charities. Nevertheless, this project was stalled because 'the Ministry of Social Solidarity

---

[36] All three interviews were conducted in September 2018.
[37] Interview, August 2018.
[38] Interview, July 2018.
[39] Interview, June 2018.
[40] Interview, June 2018.

itself is in opposition to this project, because it does not want us to cooperate with other organizations'.[41]

Even though these networks are not dense, and mainly take the form of cooperation, the simple fact that actors working in the civil society sphere know each other and cooperate together makes it ripe ground for potential mobilization. Hence, the regime ensures that the relevant ministries and/or security apparatus are always at the centre of any cooperation.

Political Opportunities and Repression

While the regime has intensified its repressive strategies through passing vague laws that legally permit increased repressive strategies against civil society actors, and by exercising control over the remaining civil society actors, twenty-one of our interviewees maintained that their organizations were able to adapt to these measures. They either found different spaces in which to work or modified their organizations' profiles in favour of economic development. Another eighteen interviewees said that they were previously members of civil society organizations engaged in development but have since turned either to social entrepreneurship or to building their own start-ups. Others apply self-censorship or self-restraint during fieldwork or field trips. 'I'm also very careful in my activities. If I want to take members on a trip, I have to think 19 times before I do, is it worth it? Will I receive the necessary security clearance?'[42] Others are vague about their work when they report it to the ministry concerned, or to the security apparatus.

> For me to continue work, I am very careful of what I say and do not say. To make sure that I do not get in trouble, I do not talk about the political problems that young people face in Egypt. I say I will talk about the problems faced by youth through arts. This is to be able to reach out to young people who need to express their feelings through art.[43]

Others claim that they are start-ups, while in reality they are NGOs:

> I'm part of a start-up that helps refugees to find employment opportunities and at other times to help others to receive scholarships abroad. We ourselves receive

---

[41] Interview, July 2018.
[42] Interview, July 2018.
[43] Interview, August 2018.

funds from XX. However, we cannot say that we are part of civil society, and our funder says that we should not mention that we are a civil society organization ... this is normal today and we all know this ... today if you say that you are part of a civil society organization and you receive funds from abroad, they accuse you of wanting to destroy the country.[44]

Another explains:

We started off as an organization to provide a space for young people to come and discuss pertinent social and economic issues, then we developed into some kind of learning institution where we provide people with various classes on how to develop a start-up. Now we have changed our organization from an NGO to a for-profit organization. This is because as an NGO we are always under the spotlight. By 2015/16 we decided to change because people started to ask about our funds and how are we able to function. Our whole work became under surveillance and it caused us a lot of problems. Hence, we decided to change to a for-profit organization.[45]

Others decided to conduct their work without publicizing it.

We are not under the spotlight, because we do not do 'campaigns' any longer. We do 'workshops', we are 'moderators' ... Honestly speaking I do not have any problems with the government or authority because I work on family planning and sexual reproductive health; perhaps this is not 'political'. However, I know of people who have many problems ... my work in public health in general, and in education, has taken me out of the spotlight, so nothing happens to me, like other people we hear about in the news.[46]

Another interviewee argued that 'during a lot of events, I do not sign any paperwork and I do not take pictures, just to make sure that I do not have anyone from the security questioning me'.[47]

Even though these activities are not in the form of mutual cooperation with other civil society organizations or by building coalition partnerships, and do not facilitate networking, they still provide some hope for the development of some independent initiatives. If and when a political opportunity develops, these civil society actors can work as a force for change. The ways in which

---

[44] Interview, August 2018.
[45] Interview, May 2018.
[46] Interview, June 2018.
[47] Interview, June 2018.

civil society actors navigate different spaces and develop new 'initiatives' and entrepreneurial opportunities are also a manifestation of the contradictions within civil society. It constitutes a power struggle between 'liberal' activists who want to promote human rights and freedoms, and the regime, yet in a symbiotic way it also links them to the regime and makes them codependent with it.

Conclusion

This chapter demonstrates how and why widespread repression increases in the polity during an authoritarian regime's transition to autocracy after regime breakdown. In contrast to the Mubarak regime's strategy of cooptation and targeted repression, the newly established regime which has been dominated by the military in 2011 culminating in the ascendence of the al-Sisi regime has been utilizing widespread repression against civil society. This shows that an authoritarian regime that breaks down after mass mobilization and is followed by an autocratization process perceives all civil society actors to be a threat to its existence. It moves first to demobilize the public through increasing repression against any potential threat or potential mobilizing activities by civil society actors, irrespective of their ideology or whether they are in the development field or not. The regime's primary concern is to ensure that all action in the public sphere is controlled and closely monitored by the security apparatus. While repression in Egypt initially started against foundations that provided foreign funding and the organizations that received these funds, later laws were intended to end civil society's independence altogether. The regime in this case instilled fear in civil society actors to stop them from engaging with the public all together. It promulgated two important laws, the NGO law and the terrorism entity law, which have legal restrictions against all sorts of civil society actors. These laws are intentionally kept vague, to provide the regime with more room for repression. This also provides civil society actors with unclear red lines, which then impact their demobilization. The establishment of government-organized non-governmental organization (GONGO)s and government-civil society partnerships is another strategy of control which the regime utilizes to control civil society actors. These strategies have impacted the extent to which civil society actors are able to work in the field, and has also impacted their decisions to either disengage from civic work altogether or to move to more 'safer' spaces like establishing business startups.

Fieldwork for this chapter shows that governments that used to support democracy promotion in the region, like the European Union and the United States, have changed course to accommodate and accept a new authoritarian regime and its repressive acts, as they perceive it as likely to protect the regional order and status quo. Unlike Jordan, which is discussed in Chapters 4 and 5, the increasing ability and willingness of the regime to use violence and repression against civil society actors has hampered the ability of the latter to develop effective campaigns promoting certain laws or progressing issues, such as legislating for street children or building hospitals.

With the increased securitization and repression in the public sphere, there was only one significant coalition-building attempt by civil society actors, mostly those that were engaged in the 'political' and human rights fields—the mobilization for the 'land', in response to Egypt's concession of the Tiran and Sanafir islands in the Red Sea to Saudi Arabia. These events, and the increase in widespread repression amalgamated with targeted repression against Islamists, mainly the Muslim Brotherhood, is discussed in Chapter 3.

Bibliography

Abdelrahman, Maha. 2015. *Egypt's Long Revolution: Protest Movements and Uprisings*. London: Routledge.

Agati, Mohamed. 2007. 'Undermining standards of good governance: Egypt's NGO law and its impact on the transparency and accountability of CSOs'. *International Journal of Not-for-Profit Law 2007* 9 (2): 56–75.

Agati, Mohamed. 2016. 'Qira'a fy qanun al-jam'iyyat al-ahliyya: Ijhad jadid: Ijhad jadid ly al-isslah [A reading of the NGO law: Another termination of reform]', *majalet al-dimuqratiyya* [*Democracy Journal*] vol. 65, (2016) online at: http://democracy.ahram.org.eg/News/12579/%D. Democracy 65: http://democracy.ahram.org.eg/News/12579/%D9%82%D8%B1%D8%A7%D8%A1%D8%A9-%D9%81%D9%89-%D9%82%D8%A7%D9%86%D9%88%D9%86-%D8%A7%D9%84%D8%AC%D9%85%D8%B9%D9%8A%D8%A7%D8%AA-%D8%A7%D9%84%D8%A3%D9%87%D9%84%D9%8A%D8%A9–%D8%A5%D8%AC%D9%87%D8%A7%D8%B6-%D8%AC%D8%AF%D9%.

Albrecht, Holger. 2005. 'How can opposition support authoritarianism? Lessons from Egypt'. *Democratization* 12 (3): 378–397.

Al-Monitor. 2019. *Egypt to amend controversial NGO law as Sisi visits Washington*. April. Accessed February 2022. https://www.al-monitor.com/originals/2019/04/sisi-visit-trump-results-new-draft-law-for-ngo-human-rights.html.

Aoudé, Ibrahim. 2013. 'Egypt: Revolutionary process and global capitalist crisis'. *Arab Studies Quarterly* 35 (3): 241–254.

Brown, Nathan, Shimaa Hatab, and Amr Adly. 2021. *Lumbering State, Restless Society: Egypt in the Modern Era*. Columbia: Columbia University Press.

Chalcraft, John. 2012. 'Horizontalism in the Egyptian revolutionary process'. *Middle East Report* 262 (42): 6–11.

Chen, XI. 2018. *Playing by the Informal Rules: Why the Chinese Regime Remains Stable Despite*. Cambridge: Cambridge University Press.

Cheskin, Ammon and Luke March. 2015. 'State–society relations in contemporary Russia: new forms of political and social contention'. *East European Politics* 31 (3): 261–273.

Christensen, Darin and Jeremy Weinstein. 2013. 'Defunding dissent: Restrictions on aid to NGOs'. *Journal of Democracy* 24 (2): 77–91.

Gervasio, Gennaro and Andrea Teti. 2020. 'Prelude to the revolution. Independent civic activists in Mubarak's Egypt and the quest for hegemony'. *Journal of North African Studies* 26 (6): 1099–1121.

Göbel, Christian. 2021. 'The Political Logic of Protest Repression in China'. *Journal of Contemporary China* 30 (128): 169–1985.

Grimm, Jannis. 2022. *Contested Legitimacies: Repression and Revolt in Post-Revolutionary Egypt*. Amsterdam: Amsterdam University Press.

Grimm, Jannis and Cilja Harders. 2018. 'Unpacking the effects of repression: the evolution of Islamist repertoires of contention in Egypt after the fall of President Morsi'. *Social Movement Studies* 17 (1): 1–18.

Hatab, Shimaa. 2018. 'Abortive regime transition in Egypt: Pro-Democracy alliance and demand-making framework'. *Democratization* 25 (4): 579–596.

Hess, David and Brian Martin. 2006. 'Repression, backfire, and the theory of transformative events'. *Mobilization* 11 (2): 249–267.

Herrold, Catherine. 2020. *Delta Democracy: Pathways to Incremental Civic Revolution in Egypt and Beyond*. Oxford: Oxford University Press.

Holmes, Amy Austin. 2019. *Coups and Revolutions: Mass Mobilization, the Egyptian Military & the United States from Mubarak to Sisi*. New York: Oxford University Press.

Honari, Ali. 2018. 'From "the effect of repression" toward "the response to repression"'. *Current Sociology Review* 66 (6): 950–973.

Human Rights Watch. 2019. *Egypt: New NGO Law Renews Draconian Restrictions: Disproportionately Huge Fines; Ban on Links with Foreign Groups*. July. Accessed February 2022. https://www.hrw.org/news/2019/07/24/egypt-new-ngo-law-renews-draconian-restrictions.

Kandil, Hazem. 2012. *Soldiers, Spies, and Statesmen: Egypt's Road to Revolt*. London: Verso.

Kandil, Hazem. 2016. *The Power Triangle: Military, Security, and Politics in Regime Change*. Oxford: Oxford University Press.

Ketchley, Neil. 2017. *Egypt in a Time of Revolution: Contentious Politics and the Arab Spring*. New York: Cambridge University Press.

Kienle, Eberhard. 2021. *Egypt: A Fragile Power*. London: Routledge.

Kurtzman, Charles. 1996. 'Structural opportunity and perceived opportunity in social-movement theory: The Iranian Revolution of 1979'. *American Sociological Review* 61: 153–170.

Li, Yao and Manfred Elfstrom. 2021. 'Does greater coercive capacity increase overt repression? Evidence from China'. *Journal of Contemporary China* 30 (128): 186–211.

Maher, Thomas V. 2010. 'Threat, resistance, and collective action: The cases of Sobibor, Treblinka and Auschwitz'. *American Sociological Review* 75 (2): 252–272.

Mansour, Sherif. 2015. *Stifling the Public Sphere: Media and Civil Society in Egypt*.

McMahon, Sean F. 2013 'Egypt's social forces, the state, and the Middle East order'. *Egypt's Tahrir Revolution*: 157–158.

Mirshak, Nadim. 2019. 'Rethinking resistance under authoritarianism: Civil society and non-contentious forms of contestation in post-uprisings Egypt'. *Social Movement Studies* 18 (6): 702–719.

Nugent, Elizabeth. 2020. *After Repression: How Polarization Derails Democratic Transition*. Princeton: Princeton University Press.

Opp, Karl-Dieter and Wolfgang Roehl. 1990. 'Repression, micromobilization, and political protest'. *Social Forces* 69 (2): 521–548.

Pearlman, Wendy. 2013. 'Emotions and the microfoundations of the Arab uprisings'. *Perspectives on Politics* 11 (2): 387–409.

Ryan, Curtis. 2001. 'Political strategies and regime survival in Egypt'. *Journal of Third World Studies* 18 (2): 25–46.

Shehata, Dina. 2011. 'The fall of the Pharaoh'. *Foreign Affairs* May/June: https://www.foreignaffairs.com/articles/middle-east/2011-06-01/fall-pharaoh.

Sika, Nadine. 2017. *Youth Activism and Contentious Politics in Egypt: Dynamics of Continuity and Change*. Cambridge: Cambridge University Press.

Sika, Nadine. 2018. 'Civil Society and the Rise of Unconventional Modes of Youth Participation in the MENA'. *Middle East Law and Governance* 10 (3): 237–263.

Sika, Nadine. 2023. *Youth in Egypt: Identity, Participation and Opportunity*. New York: New York University Press.

Springborg, Robert. 2018. 'Deep states in the MENA'. *Middle East Policy* xxv (1): 136–157.

Springborg, Robert. 2018. *Egypt*. London: Polity.

Stacher, Joshua. 2020. *Watermelon Democracy: Egypt's Turbulent Transition*. Syracuse: Syracuse University Press.

Young, Lauren. 2019. 'The psychology of state repression: Fear and dissent decisions in Zimbabwe'. *American Political Science Review* 113 (1): 140–155.

3
Activism and Demobilization in Egypt

Chapter 2 demonstrated how an authoritarian regime that breaks down and is followed by an autocratization process uses widespread repression. This chapter zooms in on the political opposition and shows how, in addition to using widespread repression against all civil society actors, targeted repression is utilized against political opposition in an effort to demobilize the public. While using targeted repression against political opposition, the regime also resorts to different modes of widespread repression against the public, especially those who are perceived as potential activists or potential participants in political dissent. Here I will examine the Egyptian regime's repressive strategies against 'politicized' civil society actors—Islamist movements, human rights organizations, independent activists, student unions, political parties, and sociopolitical movements—and the debates pertaining to the conflict–dissent nexus. These debates mainly revolve around the relation between state-led repression and public mobilization. On the one hand, scholars argue that repression can kill a movement (Davenport 2015; Chiang 2021), while on the other, that repression can motivate even more demonstrations, and that its consequences can be mixed (Lichbach 1987; Sika 2020; Davenport 2007). I will show that a regime in the process of building authoritarian control will increase its repressive tools, both widespread repression and targeted repression. Both repressive measures impact demobilization, at least during the first few years of autocratization, as they instil fear not only in the political opposition, but also in the general public and in civil society actors at large. In an effort to understand how civil society works within the confines of excessive repression, fieldwork with opposition actors is analysed. The chapter shows that when a political opportunity for mobilization opens up, activists quickly turn it to their advantage; nevertheless, mobilization under extreme repression is limited in size and short in duration.

Several laws have led to the institutionalization of repression in Egypt and granted the regime carte blanche to coerce and control political activists. Chapter 2 discussed the three major contentious events that have shaped the regime's repressive strategies towards civil society: the 25 January uprising;

the mobilization of 30 June 2013, and the Raba'a Square massacre that followed; and lastly the mobilization for the 'land'—the protests in 2017 against the decision to grant Saudi Arabia sovereignty over the islands of Tiran and Sanafir in the Straits of Tiran. In this chapter I focus only on the last two events, which illustrate the regime's use of repression against 'politicized' activists. It also sheds light on how and why activists mobilize and demobilize under high intensity repression, namely when a regime uses both widespread and targeted repression in a polity.

The Conflict–Dissent Nexus

We saw in Chapter 2 that repression is mostly enforced through the passing and institutionalization of repressive laws and by spreading fear among civil society actors. Nevertheless, when analysing the regime's tactics, we find that certain civil society activists are targeted with repression and physical force more frequently than others. As shown in the previous chapter, the literature on the conflict-dissent nexus identifies different reasons for the use of repression to demobilize the public. It is contended that authoritarian regimes utilize repression as a last resort, when all other strategies fail. Repression can also be a deterrent to further political mobilization and protests. Regimes think of the costs and benefits of repression, and how these will influence activists' ability to mobilize and/or demobilize. Hence, repression is mainly applied when a regime believes that it will demobilize the public (Chen 2018; Göbel 2021). A large body of research suggests that repression increases when the regime is directly targeted by activists (Davenport 2007). However, regime-led repression is risky because it can prompt even more demonstrations (Göbel 2021) as an unintended consequence, if a large number of people perceive the regime's use of force to be illegitimate (Opp and Roehl 1990; Grimm and Harders 2018). The case of Egypt, as a regime that foresaw breakdown followed by authoritarian regime building and autocratization suggests that repression has been used as a first resort to demobilize the public, particularly during the first few years after breakdown. As argued in Chapter 1, the escalation in violence against civil society in general, and opposition movements in particular, is exemplary of how regime building requires an excessive use of repression and coercion.

The responses to repression help to understand how it impacts demobilization in authoritarian regimes. Here, a distinction should be made between the repressive strategies that are clearly enacted by the state and those that individuals perceive to be state repression, which is 'subjective' (Kurzman 1996; Maher 2010; Honari 2018). Perceived repression negatively influences the belief in the efficacy of political participation and hence leads to demobilization. However, it can also increase grievances and stimulate further mobilization (Pearlman 2013; Honari 2018). In the case of Egypt, in an analysis of two different protest events with a different actor, one Islamist (Muslim Brotherhood) and the other secular (human rights activists, protest movement activists, independent activists, and unionists), we see harsh repression applied across the board against all political opposition. On one occasion, during the 2013 Raba'a Square massacre of Morsi's Islamist supporters by the army, there was a high incidence of physical repression, while in the second event, during the mobilization against the handing over of the Tiran and Sanafir islands, there was less physical repression in the form of killings, but severe repression through forced disappearances and imprisonments. In response, protests became shorter and localized, with fewer participants (Ketchley 2017).

The Raba'a Square Massacre

On 14 August 2013, a sit-in in Raba'a Square, in addition to one in al-Nahda Square, was mobilized by the Muslim Brotherhood and their affiliates. Negotiations between the army and the Brotherhood to disband the sit-in failed on the night of 13 August, when most of the Brotherhood leaders left the sit-in. The shooting of protesters by the military started the following morning.

> An hour into the attack, around 20 protesters lay dead. By the end of the day, there would be at least 627, according to state figures. Human Rights Watch says it documented at least 817, and suspects there may be more than 1000 ... The fragile alliance between progressives and hardliners fell apart, and Egypt was left under the influence of army chief Abdel Fatah al-Sisi. What followed was a year-long crackdown on all voices of dissent with up to 36,000 political detainees jailed.
>
> (Kingsley 2014)

Three human rights organizations investigated this massacre—Human Rights Watch, the Egyptian Initiative for Personal Rights (EIPR), and Nazra for Feminist Studies (Grimm 2022). In 2017, the website of Human Rights Watch was blocked, and EIPR's leaders were imprisoned and hit with a travel ban. Nazra's director has also been banned from travel under the non-governmental organization (NGO) foreign funding law.[1]

This event prompted a range of responses from opposition movements and activists, which further fragmented these movements between those who were in favour of using force against the sit-in and those who were against it. According to Hesham Shafick (2019, 36):

> With the exception of RevSoc [the revolutionary socialists], the general tendency, across a wide ideological spectrum, was to ignore the culpability of the state for the atrocity. While the stances of these groups on the massacre varied, they were all, with the exception of RevSoc, characterized by a common ambivalence that suggests a collective inclination across the varied components of the earlier movement.

In spite of police suppression, the National Alliance in Support of Legitimacy (NASL), a movement established by Brotherhood activists after this massacre, continued its anti-coup campaign. A limited backlash by anti-coup campaigners also took place against the security apparatus (Grimm 2022). The first reaction of Brotherhood adherents and the families of the deceased was an escalation in the number of protests during the first few days and months after these events. The security apparatus immediately intensified its crackdown on all activists. By the end of September 2013, the regime had become more violent against protesters and the Muslim Brotherhood was outlawed by the Cairo Court of Urgent Matters. This led to a wave of pre-emptive arrests and detentions, and a sharp decline in protest activities (Grimm and Harders 2018).

The first result of this massacre was to create a rift within the secular opposition, which consisted of movements, political parties, and independent activists. This broad-based opposition had been particularly influential in the years leading up to the ousting of Mubarak and in the two years following. According to one member of a protest movement:

> We coordinated between different movements, political parties, and initiatives right after Raba'a; it was mainly those who were against both the military and the Brotherhood. We kept on discussing what we should be doing and then the

---

[1] For more information on this and the cases of other human rights defenders see for instance, The International Federation for Human Rights, 'Egypt: Rejection of the appeals of Nazra for Feminist Studies and Executive Director Ms Mozn Hassan', https://www.fidh.org/en/issues/human-rights-defenders/egypt-rejection-of-the-appeals-of-nazra-for-feminist-studies-and-its; see also Human Rights Watch, 'Egypt: Events of 2020' https://www.hrw.org/world-report/2021/country-chapters/egypt#.

anniversary of January 25 came in 2014, and some wanted to mobilize and others not. The majority decided not to coordinate for mobilization; some went to the street anyway, and others went and died ... I stopped working in politics and even in civil society since December 2014 until today. This is mainly due to the closure of the public sphere ... we are very, very, very weak. We are unable to develop a strong political organization.[2]

Due to the security concerns we have, we have a lot of internal fights between our members. We are pressured all the time; we have to take tough decisions on whether we should develop a campaign or not, and due to the financial and psychological pressure, we fight a lot. This is making our work very hard. The problem is in the fact that we are unable to continue working due to the general political environment.[3]

Another activist argued that:

I worked and networked with a lot of other formal and informal organizations on public awareness campaigns for elections etc. ... However, we started to have internal problems after 30/6[4] between different groups of people working on different campaigns; after 30/6 we totally closed, and internally our relations with our members became really bad. Now there is blood, not only opinions but blood and death, with extra-judicial killings.[5]

Polarization between previous partners in opposition movements who had networked together against Mubarak has led to fragmentation and weakness. The rift between the Islamists and the secularists, in an atmosphere of heightened regime repression, has hindered the ability of the movements to mobilize large numbers or to find sympathy among bystanders (Sika 2019).

Even though the first reaction of the NASL was to mobilize against the regime, the continued repressive strategies deployed against it and against others instilled fear in many activists and their supporters. Movement fragmentation is influenced by several factors, including a dysfunctional political system, legacies of revolutionary movements, and the new political order under which a movement is formed after a revolution or uprising (Davenport 2015). Disagreements and polarization among previous coalition partners

---

[2] Interview, July 2018.
[3] Interview, July 2018.
[4] This is in reference to the coup against Morsi and the ensuing Raba'a massacre; 30 June refers to the mass demonstrations against Morsi.
[5] Interview, July 2018.

is another cause of demobilization (Pilati et al. 2023). According to Davenport (2015, 21), demobilization refers to the official termination of or significant change in the instructions which have been used to challenge authorities: the departure of members from certain organizations, mostly those who used to participate a lot; the reduction or total elimination of dissenting behaviour or protest; and lastly, the fundamental shift in activists' ideas.

Islamist Movements

Islamic associations have a long history in the Middle East and North Africa (MENA) and have gradually transformed themselves from Islamic charity organizations into formal organizations like NGOs or into movements like the Muslim Brotherhood and El Nahda (Clark 2004; Zubaida 1992; Atalay 2016). Literature on civil society, Islamic NGOs, and Islamism all use these concepts intermittently. Here I make a distinction based on Bayat's (2013) definition of Islamism as 'those ideologies and movements that strive to establish some kind of an "Islamic order"—a religious state, shari'a law, and moral codes in Muslim societies and communities' (4). This distinction is important, since Islamic charity organizations can sometimes be part of Islamist movements, like the Brotherhood or the Salafists, but can also be independent Islamist charities, or organizations developed by state institutions. Islamism has also been associated with social welfare organizations in many Middle Eastern contexts, since provision of social welfare and helping the poor is an important pillar of Islam (Clark 2012). Islamist movements have used this as a symbol of their struggle against Arab authoritarian regimes, since helping to alleviate poverty and develop social justice is implicitly addressing their regimes' inability to do so. This becomes an 'activist element of social welfare provision—putting Islam as a solution into practice—and, simultaneously, the seemingly apolitical nature of charity' (Clark 2012, 69). Thus they deliberately develop alternative institutions that differ from those of the state and represent an attractive alternative polity.

Many Islamist movements associated with the Brotherhood, for instance, adopt a Gramscian strategy for developing a moral and political hegemony in civil society, in the hope that the state will eventually become Islamic, after the Islamization of society from below through the Islamist charity organizations they have established (Bayat 2013). However, these movements, especially the Muslim Brotherhood in Egypt and in Jordan and the Islamist movements in Morocco, have been co-opted by their regimes through participating in parliamentary elections and by becoming tolerated in the public sphere throughout the 1990s and 2000s.[6] It has been argued that these movements could become moderate and reformist and be assimilated into national politics (Bayat 2013; Roy 2004). There is evidence that

> suggests that Islamism has received support from different social groups—traditional and modern, young and old, men and women, the better-off and the lower classes. But the core constituency of Islamist movements comes from the modern, educated, but often impoverished middle classes—professionals, state employees, college students and graduates.
>
> **(Bayat 2013, 6)**

> Notwithstanding their variation, Islamists in general deploy a religious language and conceptual frame, favor conservative social mores and an exclusive social order, espouse a patriarchal disposition, and adopt broadly intolerant attitudes toward different ideas and lifestyles. Theirs, then, has been an ideology and a movement that rests on a blend of religiosity and obligation, with little commitment to a language of rights—something that distinguishes it from a post-Islamist worldview.
>
> **(Ibid. 7)**

However, many other Islamist movements resort to violence against state institutions, civilians, and Western targets, to achieve their goal of an Islamic state. These movements include the Islamic Jihad and al-Jamaa al-Islamiyya in Egypt, which targeted secular intellectuals in the 1990s or have attacked Coptic Christian churches in Egypt, and hence can be termed 'un-civil' (Abdelrahman 2002).

These dual trends among Islamist civil society actors have been important in understanding state–society relations and also how the regimes use and abuse the presence of these various movements and organizations in the public sphere. At times, these movements are coopted and tolerated, as in Jordan and Morocco over the past few decades or in Egypt during the 1990s and up until the 2011 uprising, while at other times they are deemed 'terrorists' and have been cracked down upon, excluded, and repressed by their respective regimes (al-Anani 2020).

---

[6] It is important to note here that the Islamists and the Brotherhood in particular were tolerated and coopted in Egypt until 2013. For more discussion on this see, for instance, Nathan Brown, *When Victory is not an Option* (Cornell: Cornell University Press, 2012).

The Muslim Brotherhood and Repression

The Brotherhood were targeted by the Nasser regime after an incident in 1954 involving Brotherhood supporters and the police, which was followed shortly after by an assassination attempt against Nasser. In response to these events, Nasser initiated a political crackdown against all opposition, especially the Brotherhood (Nugent 2020). This culminated in the arbitrary arrest and detention of Brotherhood leaders, supporters, and rank and file members. When Sadat came to power, he changed the targets of repression from the Brotherhood to the leftists and Marxist opposition, through his so-called corrective revolution. Nevertheless, after the signing of the peace treaty with Israel and Sadat's visit to Jerusalem in 1977, the Brotherhood along with other opposition intellectuals criticized Sadat, which led to another wave of targeted repression, until Sadat's assassination in 1981 by the Islamist Jihad, who were offshoots of the Brotherhood.

During the first decade of Mubarak's rule he accommodated the Brotherhood, in line with his general policy of amnesty towards all political opposition. When the Brotherhood proved to be able to have some control over the public sphere in the 1990s through gaining power in the professional associations and syndicates, and through its ability to gain seats in parliament, the regime targeted its members (Nugent 2020). Nevertheless, during this period the Brotherhood was also accommodating and used 'non-provocative' language towards the regime. It also developed some initiatives and statements in the mid-1990s in favour of political reform, pluralism, and minority rights (al-Anani 2019).

Since the 2013 coup d'état, however, an unprecedented repressive wave against the Brotherhood has emerged. Repression against the Brotherhood has increased in both scale and degree; thousands of rank-and-file members, leaders, and even some supporters have been imprisoned. Their assets have been frozen or confiscated. Charity organizations that were associated with the Brotherhood, including educational and medical centres, have also been either shut down or confiscated by the regime. Today, the Brotherhood is considered a terrorist organization (al-Anani 2019).[7]

---

[7] It is important to note here that the research team was unable to conduct fieldwork with members of the Brotherhood, or any other Islamist organizations, since they did not agree to discuss either their work or their involvement in the public sphere.

The Institutionalization of Repression

In November 2013, a new public protest law required civil society and political actors to give the state security apparatus, mainly the Ministry of Interior, three days' notice before any protest activity. The ministry had the right to ban the demonstration or postpone it if it was deemed that it might breach the law. Later, in 2018, Law 175—the cybercrime law—was ratified by the president. It gave the regime access to all Internet users by requiring all service providers to store all users' data for 180 days. Those who did not comply could face fines of between LE 5 million and LE 10 million.[8] The law also gave the regime power to shut down any website and to develop surveillance of the population (TIMEP 2018). In addition, the terrorist entity law, the military courts law, an amendment to the penal code, and new trade union laws and labour laws were implemented, to pre-empt activists from attempting to mobilize against the regime (Holmes 2019). The terrorist entity law, enforced in August 2015, was used against different media outlets and offered impunity to security personnel as well as to the military in their war on terror (Human Rights Watch (HRW) 2015). These laws, in addition to the NGO law discussed in Chapter 2, have been the basis for the institutionalization of repression and for embedding the new authoritarian regime in Egypt since 2013. The Ministry of Justice has been instrumental in justifying state-led violence through endorsing mass death sentences, which reached an unprecedented high in 2014. In only four months, 1,212 individuals were sentenced to death by the courts (Holmes 2019).

Repression and Demobilization

In response to activists' ability to mobilize for large-scale protests,[9] the regime increased its repression against other political actors and students as well. From the regime's perspective, all of them were activists or organizations that were most likely to mobilize. Student activists and student unions also became targets of repression. The Islamists in general and the Brotherhood in particular have had a strong presence in public universities since the 1970s, when Sadat allowed them more freedom of representation in the

---

[8] By May 2022 this had risen from almost US$320,000 to US$640,000.
[9] This is a result of movements' abilities to mobilize, especially Tamarrod, a grassroots movement that was allegedly able to gather more than 10 million signatures against Morsi and to mobilize in public protests. In addition, the Islamists' ability to retain some mobilizational momentum after Raba'a, in spite of repression, is another factor.

public sphere to counter the power of the Nasserists and Marxists on campus.[10] When students in public universities developed a group called Students against the Coup, university security cracked down on them and the group was dismantled. Other politically active students in public universities were targeted, and student union elections were blocked (Holmes 2019). Student union activities have become increasingly restricted since 2013, and more so every year. An interviewee argued that 'now, it was very hard from a security perspective to bring in any visitors from outside. ... I had so many hopes and dreams and I thought I could change a lot. Unfortunately, my experience in the union changed me from being an optimistic to a pessimistic person.'[11] Another explained that:

> My university is considered a 'border university' and hence the military interfered a lot in our affairs. After June 30, everything shut down. Our university president is a politician par excellence. During the 2013 elections, I could not forget how everything had changed. A new rule was established, which says that no one who is politically active or belongs to any political group or religious group could run for elections. Of course, it was written in such a way that a large number of student contestants were pushed out of the race.[12]

'Any political activity, sit-in or even a sit-in against a university policy, not [even a national] policy in Egypt is banned.'[13] 'In 2015 there was tight security on campus; no one was allowed in from outside if they were not affiliated with the university.'[14]

> We used to do a lot of activities, but for the past four years, i.e. since 2014, we are not allowed to do anything; even bike riding is banned. I am not sure why ... if it is because of the high cost of bikes, or if it is due to security concerns. Here at our university, it is forbidden to talk about politics. So, we cannot hold any event that talks about politics. One time a 'family' [student group] which is a student club was stopped because they held an event that hinted at political issues.[15]

Protest movement actors and political party members belonging to the secular opposition were also targeted. Our research group reached out to more than thirty activists from different opposition political parties and protest

---

[10] For more discussion on this see Nadine Sika. 2023. *Youth in Egypt: Identity, Participation and Opportunity*. New York, New York University Press, ch. 3.
[11] Interview, June 2018.
[12] Interview, June 2018.
[13] Interview, July 2018.
[14] Interview, July 2018.
[15] Interview, June 2018.

movements, as well as independent activists. Only six agreed to be interviewed, three of whom had disengaged from political life in reaction to the increased repression. One admitted that 'I was a member of a political party that is being established, whose paperwork is under investigation, but one of the main reasons why in 2014 I left political life and civic engagement was because of the political sphere's closure'.[16] Political parties, mainly those belonging to the political opposition, were also targeted by the regime:

> Today we have some sort of political closure, especially on political parties in general, but in particular on political parties that could be called 'opposition front'. There is no secure political work. Anyone working on political issues can be called a security risk; for instance, one of our colleagues [just] came out of prison, thank God. But in 2018, right before Ramadan, one of our other colleagues was sentenced to three years but came out of jail during the presidential amnesty. We are under pressure, even though we are not a revolutionary political party. ... Many of our members have quit.[17]

Members of opposition political parties, both from the left, like the Bread and Freedom Party, or Islamist reformers from the right like the Strong Egypt Party, were allowed to have many adherents. Members of their executive committees were part of the same social network and were also part of the same protest movements. They were able to mobilize different stakeholders onto the streets in the months leading to the 2013 coup, which influenced the regime's perception of threat from these activists.

> I used to be a member of a political party and in different presidential campaigns for XX political party. However, after 2013 I stopped all political activities, since I received a threat to my life and a threat to my family, so I quit all political work. I do not even talk politics on Facebook any longer. Now I turn to civil society organizations only, and to charity work. The charity organization I am part of today is for orphanages and the poor, in addition to helping needy families who have members with cancer.

Another interviewee explained:

> I was a member of the NDP [National Democratic Party under Mubarak] and then I was part of the XX campaign and then went to XX political party. In January 2011 I was one of the founding members of XX party. Now I work in civil society on youth

---

[16] Interview, July 2018.
[17] Interview, July 2018.

and women's empowerment. When I was a member of XX party, we were used to having security closures, so to do any events, we were better off being a 'civil society' organization than political party ... and after June 30 everything closed. Even the organization we built as a civil society organization was shut down .... They [security] did not shut us down, but people stopped attending our events. After June 2013, the international funders with whom we worked stopped funding us, since our main work was on political empowerment.[18]

Another one said that: 'I used to work for a political party and was also a member of this party. However, with the recent events and problems I left political life altogether'.[19]

Human rights activists have been targeted through imprisonment, threat of imprisonment, or simply by travel bans. One interviewee told us that:

I work at a XX legal office. I was on my way to Lebanon and my colleague was on his way to Morocco, and on December 5, 2014, we found out that we were both banned from traveling under the NGO foreign funding law, case number 17 of 2011. During the same time the media machine was against all human rights organizations, and after June 30 our office was considered to be affiliated with the 'April 6' movement even though we had no members of this movement in our office.[20]

The increase in the regime's repressive activities against activists impacted not only their ability to mobilize for street demonstrations, but also their ability to form coalition partnerships and networks. In addition, the virtual end of financial support for democracy by international donors also affected activists' participation. Many scholars have analysed how democracy promotion can help authoritarian regimes to embed their power instead of democratizing (Carapico 2014; Durac and Cavatorta 2009), while others have discussed the importance of such aid for democracy promotion (Knack 2004; Allison and Beschel 1992). Nevertheless, the fact that democracy promotion and democracy aid are part of a diplomatic relationship between the donors and the recipient regimes leads to a neglect of civil society actors. Fieldwork with activists demonstrates that democracy promotion programmes are merely a reflection of 'the strategic interests shared by both donor and recipient state, as well as how each perceives the ability of the other to advance its interests' (Snider 2018, 796). Thus when a strategic

---

[18] Interview, July 2018.
[19] Interview, June 2018.
[20] Interview, July 2018.

authoritarian regime constricts civil society, international donors stop their activities, putting human rights and democracy on hold.

For almost three years after the Raba'a massacre, the regime managed to shut down all political opportunities and to threaten activists with repression. However, in April 2016, when the regime disclosed information about the handover of the Red Sea islands of Tiran and Sanafir to Saudi Arabia, mobilization and demonstrations erupted. This time, however, there was no mass mobilization, only sporadic demonstrations in downtown Cairo, and none in Tahrir Square.

The Tiran and Sanafir Controversy

Small protests took place in different parts of the country after Friday prayers but were quickly dispersed by security forces. The largest demonstration was at Egypt's press syndicate in central Cairo, where several thousand protesters gathered, according to Ahram Online reporters, making it the largest such protest in recent months. The protesters chanted against the decision but also used slogans familiar from the January 2011 revolution, such as 'bread, freedom and social justice' and 'the people want the regime to fall'. One chant was 'bread, freedom and those islands are Egyptian' (Ahram Online 2016). Activists called for more protests the following week, on 25 April, 2016, which was the anniversary of the liberation of Sinai.

More than ninety people were arrested between 21 April and 24 in the lead-up to the planned protests, according to figures released by Egyptian human rights organizations and Freedom for the Brave. Many of those arrested were remanded in custody on multiple charges, including breaching the counter-terrorism law, the protest law, and other laws regulating public assemblies, as well as for 'national security' offences under the penal code (Amnesty International 2016).

Furthermore, the regime stormed the press syndicate during the demonstrations and more than 500 websites were later blocked by the security apparatus. By 2017, the leadership of the human rights movement was either subjected to asset freezes or travel bans (Holmes 2019, 203). According to an interviewee's account, 'In 2015 and 2016 all political figures who were in charge of mobilization against Tiran and Sanafir were imprisoned … all of them except myself. To be frank, I fled and went to Upper Egypt, then I returned on April 25 to the demonstration site to be able to organize it … I walked without a phone or anything.'[21]

---

[21] Interview, July 2018.

In the weeks leading up to the demonstrations, activists were able to mobilize on a small scale. An activist explained that:

> For Tiran and Sanafir we organized ourselves, but it was not only XX as a movement, it was independent activists as well; we all worked together … we coordinated with XX and XX. … The problem is that the media is now showing us as individuals who want to destroy the country. … I have colleagues who have 20 to 30 years of prison sentences. … This is unfair … [on the] Friday of the Land [protests] and the Friday before, there were very many people. Therefore, since then, repression has been unprecedented … if they used to hit us with an iron fist before, now, after Tiran and Sanafir, they use even harsher measures with all their repressive capacities.[22]

Another activist commented that 'since Tiran and Sanafir they [the regime] increased their security, and they want to send the message that whoever talks will not get out of prison. Even those who were able to get out of prison had to pay large bails. They [the regime] were shocked that we were still able to mobilize, so as a consequence, they increased their repressive measures'.[23] Another activist recounts that the days leading to the demonstrations:

> When I came out of the metro station in Dokki [a suburb in west Cairo], I was taken from there. I had not even demonstrated and did not participate in anything. I went to prison for almost 24 hours, and after we were interrogated, we went to another place for three days, and then they left me. Then I had a prison sentence of five years and a LE 100,000 fine. At this time, I and other people with me were accused of things we did not do. After I appealed, and spent six or seven months in prison, I was let go, but I had to pay LE 50,000. I really did not know anything or anyone, I just went downtown to see what was happening. … The demonstration law is the main reason why I was imprisoned. … Now I am not interested in politics at all. It is over; let them do whatever they want to do, I do not care.[24]

Pre-emptive repressive strategies like these arouse fear in a large number of activists, and instead of further mobilization, they demobilized and/or disengaged from political life. A member of a political party explains that:

---

[22] Interview, July 2018.
[23] Interview, July 2018.
[24] Interview, June 2018.

> Today we have political closure on political parties in general, but political parties that are part of an opposition coalition. There is no secure political work; anyone working on political issues is under attack. For instance, one of our colleagues was released from prison right before Ramadan in 2018. Another colleague was sentenced to three years, yet was released after a presidential pardon. We are under pressure, even though we are not a revolutionary political party. ... Many of our members have decided to quit as a consequence.[25]

Another former member of a protest movement recalled that 'there was a time when I was studying abroad in 2015 or 2016 when I deleted all my social media accounts before returning to Egypt. I was afraid to that extent, and this is based on the extent to which they [the regime] started to round people up based on their Facebook profiles'.[26]

It is apparent that state-led repression is capable of demobilizing activism in the short term. Even when mobilization occurs, pre-emptive repression instils fear and discourages further large-scale mobilization. Nevertheless, some activists see this increase in repression as a sign of regime weakness. One interviewee argued that: 'The security forces have a big crisis which is that they do not know the power of the people in front of them. i.e. some groups or individuals might not have any power to do anything and they imagine that they have the power to mobilize and do extraordinary things. So they repress anyone they encounter'.[27]

Activists' responses, demobilization, and perception of regime repression bring us back to the central dilemma of how repression impacts dissent. On the one hand, activists seem to 'perceive' the regime's repressive strategies to be very powerful, and to fear them. However, some of these activists also believe that high repression is a result of the regime's weakness. This is also related to whether activists were exposed to repression themselves, or only 'perceive' this repression against others. According to research on the former USSR (Union of Soviet Socialist Republics), only those groups that were exposed to extreme repression by Stalin behaved more loyally to the regime. Nevertheless, these same citizens were the first to demonstrate and to oppose the regime when a political opportunity presented itself and when the regime's repression decreased (Rozenas and Zhukov 2019). For the past decade, the regime in Egypt has been able to utilize repression against civil society actors in order to demobilize the public. And so far, the rise in repression has been successful in pre-empting large-scale mobilizations.

---

[25] Interview, July 2018.
[26] Interview, June 2018.
[27] Interview, July 2018.

Conclusion

The two contentious events described previously have demonstrated the rise in the use of repressive strategies by the regime towards political activists, which has led many of them to disengage fully from politics. In the process of targeting political activists, the regime also uses widespread repression against any passer-by near a demonstration site. This instils fear in the general public, preempting them from participating in any potential opposition activity. Activists' inability to mobilize, organize, or even when organized, to draw large numbers of supporters, has also affected demobilization. Even though no specific movement was identified, except for the Brotherhood, the chapter discussed how actors within different movements, parties or human rights organizations have either withdrawn from activism completely or changed their activities from 'political' to 'social'. In this case, we see that opposition actors and movements have been 'killed' from the outside through an increase in targeted repression, which ultimately affected their ability to sustain their work. Resource deprivation becomes another problem for these activists and movements, especially when funding stops or is impossible to attract, and hence there is insufficient basis for organization and to sustain the work (Davenport 2015). The case of human rights organizations is important in this regard, since foreign funds are becoming hard to attract. In addition, foreign funders become complicit in this resource deprivation, since they stop their funding to human rights organizations in order to prevent 'political' friction with 'friendly' autocrats. Scholars like Olson (1965) and Davenport (2015) argue that repression increases fear among activists, who do not want to be subjected to physical harm or harassment. Hence, to avoid these actions, activists demobilize. Although this argument is not accepted by some scholars, who believe that repression can provoke dissent, in the case of Egypt during the height of repressive strategies, repression, both widespread against all civil society actors and targeted against political opposition and human rights actors, did indeed stop dissent in the decade following the 2013 coup d'état (Carey 2006; Weede 1987; Davenport 2015).

Bibliography

Abdelrahman, Maha. 2002. 'The politics of "uncivil" society in Egypt'. *Review of African Political Economy* 29 (91): 21–35.

Ahram Online. 2016. *Protests in Egypt against Red Sea Islands Deal, More expected on 25 April.* 15 April. Accessed 15 February 2022. https://english.ahram.org.eg/

NewsContent/1/64/199636/Egypt/Politics-/Update—Protests-in-Egypt-against-Red-Sea-islands-.aspx.

Allison, Graham and Robert Jr. Beschel. 1992. 'Can the United States promote democracy?' *Political Science Quarterly* 107 (1): 81–98.

al-Anani, Khalil. 2020. 'Devout Neoliberalism?! Explaining Egypt's Muslim brotherhood's socio-economic perspective and policies'. *Politics and Religion* 13 (4): 748–767.

Amnesty International. 2016. 'Egypt: Mass arrests in "ruthlessly efficient" bid to block peaceful protest'. 26 April. Accessed 15 February 2022. https://www.amnesty.org/en/latest/news/2016/04/egypt-mass-arrests-in-ruthlessly-efficient-bid-to-block-peaceful-protest/.

Atalay, Zeynep. 2016. 'Vernacularization of liberal civil society by transnational Islamist NGO networks'. *Global Networks* 16 (3): 1470–2266.

Bayat, Asef. 2013. 'Post-Islamism at large'. In *Post-Islamism: The Changing Faces of Political Islam*, by Asef Bayat, 3–34. Oxford: Oxford University Press.

Carapico, Sheila. 2014. *Political Aid and Arab Activism: Democracy Promotion, Justice and Representation*. Cambridge: Cambridge University Press.

Carey, Sabine. 2006. 'The dynamic relationship between protest and repression'. *Political Research Quarterly* 59 (1): 1–11.

Chen, Xi. 2018. *Playing by the Informal Rules: Why the Chinese Regime Remains Stable Despite*. Cambridge: Cambridge University Press.

Chiang, Amy Yunyu. 2021. 'Violence, non-violence and the conditional effect of repression on subsequent dissident mobilization'. *Conflict Management and Peace Science* 38 (6): 627–653.

Clark, Janine A. 2004. *Islam, Charity, and Activism: Middle-Class Networks and Social Welfare in Egypt, Jordan, and Yemen*. Bloomington: Indiana University Press.

Clark, Janine. 2012. 'Patronage, prestige, and power: The Islamic Center Charity Society's political role within the Muslim Brotherhood'. In *Islamist Politics in the Middle East: Movements and Change*, by Samer Shehata, 68–88. London: Routledge.

Davenport, Christian. 2007. 'State repression and political order'. *Annual Review of Political Science* 10: 1–23.

Davenport, Christian. 2009. 'Regimes, repertoires and state repression'. *Swiss Political Science Review* 15 (2): 377–385.

Davenport, Christian. 2015. *How Social Movements Die: Repression and Demobilization of the Republic of New Africa*. Cambridge, MA: Cambridge University Press.

Durac, Vincent and Francesco Cavatorta. 2009. 'Strengthening authoritarian rule through democracy promotion? Examining the paradox of the US and EU security strategies: The case of Bin Ali's Tunisia'. *British Journal of Middle Eastern Studies* 36 (1): 3–19.

Göbel, Christian. 2021. 'The political logic of protest repression in China'. *Journal of Contemporary China* 30 (128): 169–1985.

Grimm, Jannis. 2022. *Contested Legitimacies: Repression and Revolt in Post-Revolutionary Egypt*. Amsterdam: Amsterdam University Press.

Grimm, Jannis and Cilja Harders. 2018. 'Unpacking the effects of repression: The evolution of Islamist repertoires of contention in Egypt after the fall of President Morsi'. *Social Movement Studies* 17 (1): 1–18.

Holmes, Amy Austin. 2019. *Coups and Revolutions: Mass Mobilization, the Egyptian Military & the United States from Mubarak to Sisi*. New York: Oxford University Press.

Honari, Ali. 2018. 'From "the effect of repression" toward "the response to repression"'. *Current Sociology Review* 66 (6): 950–973f.

Ketchley, Neil. 2017. *Egypt in a Time of Revolution: Contentious Politics and the Arab Spring*. Cambridge: Cambridge University Press.

Kingsley, Patrick. 2014. *The Guardian Egypt's Rabaa massacre: One year on*. August 16. Accessed 13 February 2022. https://www.theguardian.com/world/2014/aug/16/rabaa-massacre-egypt-human-rights-watch.

Knack, Stephen. 2004. 'Does foreign aid promote democracy?' *International Studies Journal* 48: 251–266.

Kurzman, Charles. 1996. 'Structural opportunity and perceived opportunity in social-movement theory: The Iranian revolution of 1979'. *American Sociological Review* 61: 153–170.

Lichbach, Mark Irving. 1987. 'Deterrence or escalation? The puzzle of aggregate studies of repression and dissent'. *Journal of Conflict Resolution* 31 (2): 266–297.

Maher, Thomas V. 2010. 'Threat, resistance, and collective action: The cases of Sobibor, Treblinka and Auschwitz'. *American Sociological Review* 75 (2): 252–272.

Mirshak, Nadim. 2019. 'Rethinking resistance under authoritarianism: Civil society and non-contentious forms of contestation in post-uprisings Egypt'. *Social Movement Studies* 18 (6): 702–719.

Nugent, Elizabeth. 2020. *After Repression: How Polarization Derails Democratic Transition*. Princeton: Princeton University Press.

Olson, Mancur. 1965. *The Logic of Collective Action*. Cambridge: Harvard University Press.

Pearlman, Wendy. 2013. 'Emotions and the microfoundations of the Arab uprisings'. *Perspectives on Politics* 11 (2): 387–409.

Opp, Karl-Dieter and Wolfgang Roehl. 1990. 'Repression, micromobilization, and political protest'. *Social Forces* 69 (2): 521–548.

Pilati, Katia, Giuseppe Acconcia, David Leone Suber, and Henda Chennaoui. 2023. 'Protest demobilization in post-revolutionary settings: Trajectories to counter-revolution and to democratic transition'. *Political Studies* 71 (3): 634–654. https://doi.org/10.1177/00323217211034050.

Roy, Olivier. 2004. *Globalized Islam: The Search for a New Ummah*. New York: Columbia University Press.

Rozenas, Arturas and Yuri Zhukov. 2019. 'Mass repression and political loyalty: Evidence from Stalin's terror by hunger'. *American Political Science Review* 113 (2): 5690–5583.

Shafick, Hesham. 2019. 'Acts of ignorance: How could Egypt's revolutionaries overlook a state massacre of 1000+ protestors?' *Interface: A Journal for and about Social Movements* 11 (2): 35–62.

Sika, Nadine. 2019. 'Repression, cooptation and movement fragmentation: Evidence from the Youth Movement in Egypt'. *Political Studies* 67 (3): 676–692.

Sika, Nadine. 2020. 'Contentious activism and political trust in non-democratic regimes: Evidence from the MENA'. *Demcoratiztion* 27 (8): 1515–1532.

Sika, Nadine. forthcoming. *Youth in Contemporary Egypt: The Promise, the Peril and the Poor*. New York: New York University Press.

Snider, Erin. 2018. 'Democracy aid and the authoritarian state: Evidence from Egypt and Morocco'. *International Studies Quarterly* 62: 795–808.

The Tahrir Institute for Middle East Policy TIMEP. 2018. *TIMEP Brief: Cybercrime Law Egypt*. 19 December. Accessed 13 February 2022. https://timep.org/reports-briefings/cybercrime-law-brief/.

Weede, Erich. 1987. 'The rise of the West to Eurosclerosis: Are there lessons for the Asian-Pacific region?' *Asian Culture Quarterly* 15 (1): 1–14.

Zubaida, Sami. 1992. 'Islam, the state and democracy'. *Middle East Report* 179 (November/December 1992). https://merip.org/1992/11/islam-the-state-and-democracy/

4
Political Context, Co-Optation, and Targeted Repression in Jordan

The authoritarian regime in Jordan has survived different political threats, and its authoritarian institutions have remained resilient, even while other authoritarian regimes in the region have broken down. To understand how and why targeted repression is mostly utilized against political opposition, while other civil society actors are tolerated, this chapter looks at the historical context. This context helps us understand the period in which certain events occur, and the interpretations of these events, in order to help identify the accumulation of cultural, social, political, and even geographic processes which shape collective action (Tilly and Tarrow 2006; Ancelovici 2021). Contextualizing specific events gives insight into state–society relations in one setting versus another (Falleti and Lynch 2009; Ancelovici 2021). In Jordan, the role of the tribal elders, and society at large in instigating and also in constraining dissent is essential, and hence understanding how social forces add to demobilization in authoritarian contexts is important in understanding how and why concession and targeted repression work under certain circumstances. Thus in this chapter, I draw on Ancelovici's model, which looks at both the political and the non-political spheres. According to this model, society has various fields that encompass different opportunities—the 'field opportunity structure' (Ancelovici 2021). This model adds a non-state sphere to the political opportunity structure. It demonstrates that society itself has different fields encompassing different opportunities, and that this sometimes helps activists in their mobilization efforts, while at other times it constrains them.

The development of contentious activities can be associated with a change in the structure of the prevailing opportunities. When such an opportunity arises, it increases the capacity of actors to change (Ancelovici 2021; Tarrow 1996, 1998). This puts the state at the centre of the dynamics, which is important for certain civil society actors. For other civil society actors, however, the society at large plays an important role. In this chapter and Chapter 5, I will draw on the fact that society in general can also add to the constraints which civil society actors can experience. In this chapter I analyse the political and historical context in Jordan to better understand how political opportunities and threats have framed the interplay between political liberalization and concessions on the one hand and targeted repressive measures on the other. Unlike the case of Egypt, where widespread and targeted repression have been utilized to demobilize the public, this chapter shows that in the case of Jordan, the regime relies on other authoritarian tools—mainly concessions and targeted repression—for demobilization. It demonstrates how these have shaped civil society in Jordan and its ability to mobilize for change. My analysis is based on the relational and interactionist approach to social movements, which focuses on the micro and macro contexts (Volpi and Clark 2019; Cavatorta and Clark 2022).

I analyse three contentious events—one historical, and two more recent. The first event is Black September of 1970, which has been seminal for Jordan's state- and regime-building process ever since (Lucas 2008). The second event is the demonstrations of 2011 associated with the Arab uprisings in the region, and the third is the Dawar Rabe' (Fourth Circle) event of 2018. To what extent does the Jordanian regime utilize targeted repression towards political activists? How do activists respond to this? We will see that the regime uses concessions most of the time, while targeted repression is utilized against opposition activists who are perceived to be a threat to the regime. Civil society activists, on the other hand, are capable of turning the political context to their own advantage in order to mobilize for some socioeconomic and political change. Yet civil society is also constrained by both political and field opportunities within a polity, and hence when targeted repression increases, activists demobilize in response.

The Repression–Concession Nexus

The repression–concession nexus has been an important aspect of social movement studies. This relationship has an interactive influence on social movements and protest activities. According to Goldstone and Tilly (2001), political threats are a combination of a regime's utilization of both repression and concessions to influence mobilization and contentious activities. This combination can effectively reduce opposition (Davenport 2009; Yuen and Cheng 2017). Authoritarian regimes choose to tolerate protest activities at some times, ignore them at others, or repress them at still others (Yuen and Cheng 2017; Bishara 2014; Moss 2014).

The political process approach argues that there are certain opportunities that are not necessarily formal or permanent in the political context which can act as incentives for contentious activities. Here, we see how different factors can either increase or decrease the cost of collective action.

Scholars distinguish between different types of targeted repression. For instance, a regime may use surveillance against activists while provoking them to stop their political activism. It may also increase censorship and reduce activists' access to certain sources. The websites of social movements can be shut down or hacked if and when activists resort to oppositional mobilization. By withholding or depriving a movement of recognition, the regime tacitly utilizes repression. Verbally threatening activists is another method, as is creating counter-mobilizations against a particular movement and/or demand in order to repress opposition movements. Finally, physical harm or the threat of it may be applied, in an attempt to confine activists by banning them from travel or forcing them into exile (Moss 2014). But as argued previously, repression is costly and not always successful, and regimes therefore use other techniques, mainly concessions (in the form of material and political rights) to retain power. Material concessions include but are not limited to spending on health and education and even on individual members of the opposition. The political rights concession includes opening up political space to give the opposition some opportunities to participate beyond the regime's control (Conrad 2011). Jordan is an example of a regime utilizing targeted repression as well as concessions, and these two strategies have shaped contentious politics, mobilization, and demobilization in the Hashemite Kingdom.

Black September and Its Consequences

The events of September 1970, known as Black September, were decisive in defining the Jordanian regime, the rules and strategies established afterwards by King Hussein, and how state–society relations have unfolded until today. The roots of this event lie in the confrontation between the Palestinian Liberation Organization (PLO) and its various factions, mainly Fatah and the fedayeen armed militia, vis-à-vis the Jordanian regime. The beginning of this confrontation can be traced back to the defeat of the Arab states in the 1967 war and Israel's subsequent takeover of the West Bank. After 1967, the fedayeen assumed many governmental functions in Jordan. They set up a jurisdiction intended to develop into a parallel government, undermining the power and legitimacy of the monarchy. They also participated in the elections of the trade union federation, supporting the unions' demands against those of the Jordanian regime. In the summer of 1970, a Fatah spokesman raised the idea of a Palestinian revolution instead of Palestinian resistance (al-Majaly 2003). This was a none-too-subtle threat directed at the Jordanian regime and showed that the Palestinian struggle was no longer only to liberate Palestine or to destroy Israel; it had become a revolutionary ideological struggle against a 'conservative' monarchical regime, with the goal of a 'revolution', implying an intention to change the regime in Amman as well. The events that followed have been described as 'violent coexistence' (Nevo 2008, 222).[1] In September 1970 there was an alleged assassination attempt on King Hussein, which led to an armed confrontation between the two sides. This event was in effect a civil war; the Jordanian army crushed an armed insurrection by the Palestinian fedayeen in a conflict that cost almost ten thousand lives (Yom 2009).

Balancing Targeted Repression and Concession after Black September

This conflict was a vital first step in establishing a distinct Jordanian identity, as opposed to a Palestinian identity. It began an era of 'Jordanization' of the government, the military, and the public sector, which had been hegemonized by Palestinians. The role of the secret services—the *mukhabarat*—increased as a result. They are believed to be the main protectors of Jordanian identity, and hence the most suitable body to fend off Palestinian 'penetration' of society and politics (Gallets 2015). In addition, the presence and functions of East Bank Jordanians increased. Their numbers grew in the state bureaucracy, security services, and the military. A new political party, the Jordanian National Union, was founded as a hegemonic political party, to form a popular support base for the regime. This party was the only functioning legal political organization in the country, since all political parties had been banned in 1957 (Lucas 2008). The Jordanian National Union became a platform for many different political trends, however. Ideological diversity

---

[1] See for instance interview with former Jordanian Prime Minister, Abdel Azim Al-Majaly, with al-Araby, online at: https://www.youtube.com/watch?v=ZyKUo_L7n4U; See also al-Quds al-Araby, 'Nazir Rashid mudir al-mukhabarat al-'urduniyya al-sabiq fy mudhakaraty'. [Nazir Rashid former Director of Jordanian Intelligence in his biography], 9 December 2006. https://www.alquds.co.uk/%D9%86%D8%B0%D9%8A%D8%B1-%D8%B1%D8%B4%D9%8A%D8%AF-%D9%85%D8%AF%D9%8A%D8%B1-%D8%A7%D9%84%D9%85%D8%AE%D8%A7%D8%A8%D8%B1%D8%A7%D8%AA-%D8%A7%D9%84%D8%A7%D8%B1%D8%AF%D9%86%D9%8A%D8%A9-%D8%A7%D9%84%D8%B3-2/.

was absent, since King Hussein sought to impose uniformity over all political ideologies, ranging from conservative to leftist. As a further step in Jordanization, the king cut all administrative ties to the West Bank. This step had the unintended consequence of fuelling the economic crisis facing the regime. Subsidies on a number of products were removed, prompting large-scale demonstrations in 1989 which are referred to as the Jordanian Intifada (Abu Khusa 1991; Lucas 2005; Ryan 2018).

Historically, especially after Black September, the regime developed coalitions with several major partners who have become the backbone of its survivability and legitimacy. The most important coalition partner is the East Bank tribes, whose members have been assigned to jobs in most state and bureaucratic sectors. The second important coalition partners are the religious and ethnic minorities, mainly the Christians, Circassians, and Chechens. These minorities also fill different state positions to ensure that they feel included in the polity. The third and fourth coalition partners are the state bureaucracy and the military; the development of these institutions over the years has led to the creation of distinct institution identities that go beyond members' tribal or ethnic affiliations. The fifth coalition partner, despite the Black September events, is the Palestinians, particularly those working in the private sector who own large, successful businesses, as well as those 1948 Palestinian refugees who were able to improve their socioeconomic status through circular migration to the Gulf, and the West Bank elites who allied themselves with the Jordanian regime during the latter's control of the West Bank (Brand 1994; Lucas 2005; Clark 2012). These elites have been favoured and have held key political positions, in addition to participating in the army and civil bureaucracy (Masaad 2001). These coalitions and partnerships have been a double-edged sword, however. On the one hand, they have strengthened state legitimacy and influenced Jordan's political identity. On the other, these same coalitions and partnerships functioned as a pre-emptive strategy to contain and weaken any real opposition against the regime (Clark 2012).

A New Wave of Contentious Events

In April 1989, it was these same coalition partners who began the demonstrations against the regime. The mobilization began in the city of Ma'an in Southern Jordan, an area traditionally a major pillar of support for the regime, and whose citizens were part of the East Bank military and political leadership. However, it was rank-and-file East Bankers who relied on fixed incomes from the government who were the ones to demonstrate. Protesters called for both economic and political reforms (al-Manaseer 2011). 'The protesters voiced their support for the monarchy as an institution but called for returning the subsidies, new parliamentary elections, and the sacking of Prime Minister Zayd al-Rifa'i' (Lucas 2005, 27). The first reaction of the government was to repress protestors, while ten of the eleven labour unions in Jordan supported the demonstrations. The government of Zaid al-Rifa'i resigned in response to the mounting demonstrations (al-Manaseer 2011).

In the meanwhile, instead of resorting to widespread repression and force against demonstrators, the regime chose to liberalize the polity (Lucas 2005). The regime has always held the upper hand in Jordan, co-opting some and excluding others, at the same time as dividing and coercing. It now resorted to various co-optation strategies and opened the way for political contestation and parliamentary elections. The discussions on drafting a National Charter were directed mainly at the opposition groups which the regime regarded as co-optable. Some 'radical' opposition groups like Hizb al-Tahrir were excluded from these discussions. The major rules of engagement and charter provisions were laid out by the regime, not by opposition leaders. It was implicitly agreed that the political opposition would accept the legitimacy of the regime and the monarchy in return for an opening of the political sphere (Lucas 2008). Laws restricting personal and political liberties, and the emergency and martial laws, were revoked. A new law on publications increased press freedoms and brought a proliferation of daily and weekly independent press and media outlets (Lucas 2008; Salameh 2017). More importantly, political parties were allowed to become part of the public sphere and parliamentary elections were held (Lucas 2012; Salameh 2017). In the meantime, the regime ensured that even if a strong opposition was present in the legislature, it would not be able to pass legislation that would adversely affect the regime's power. For instance, members of the lower house have to be approved by a majority of upper house members, who are appointed by the king (Schwedler 2006). In 1989 the Muslim Brotherhood performed well, winning 27% of parliamentary seats (Lucas 2005). The tribal independents received the largest share, not only in this parliament but in all previous and subsequent parliaments, since they compete for the votes of their tribes based on their ability to provide services and employment opportunities to their tribal constituencies (Clark 2018). The earlier liberalization, combined with the co-optation of these tribes, seems to have also changed the social and political practices of the tribes. For instance, they created primaries to select their own candidates for parliamentary elections after the changes of 1989. These elections in and of themselves have undermined the power of the powerful, elderly tribal leadership and have empowered younger tribesmen who are better educated and have more knowledge, work experience, and political know-how as a result of their experience cooperating with state officials (Brand 1994). Even though these measures are important, activists have argued that they are not enough, and that the majority of these reforms are cosmetic. Nevertheless, they believe that their situation and the freedoms they enjoy compare favourably to those in other countries in the region. 'We do not have many freedoms, but compared to other countries we are very good'.[2] This perception can also function as a legitimation strategy, as citizens compare themselves to others in similar situations and conclude they are better off under their regime than others under similar regimes.

The Co-Optation of Political Parties

Political parties have been constructed to have minimal influence in the public sphere, with many constraining laws. Yet political parties dominate the opposition political spectrum. They vary from pro-monarchy, conservative political parties to Arab nationalists, leftists, and Islamists. The loyalist, conservative political parties support the East Bank nationalist sentiments and support the monarchy. These parties are able to secure a large number of legislative seats; however, they are organizationally weak and do not have much public support, apart from their own constituents in the East Bank. In addition, they do not have a clear ideological or political programme. The leftists and the pan-Arab nationalist parties were strong during the early years of Jordan's liberalization process in the 1950s, and they were mainly linked to the West Bank and the Palestinians. These groups reflected a major opposition to the monarchy, and they were powerful, as they had the support of nationalists in other countries in the region such as Egypt. After the 1967 defeat, however, these parties lost much of their popular support and ability to mobilize (Lust-Okar 2001).

By contrast, the Islamists, mainly the Islamic Action Front, have enjoyed much support in Jordanian politics. One of the main reasons why they were influential and had much support is that they were never banned from politics. The group is registered as a social organization, not a political party, and hence when political parties were outlawed, the front was still existent in

---

[2] Interview, November 2018.

the public sphere through other means. In addition, since they have historically supported the monarchy and demonstrated their loyalty to it, they have been tolerated (Lust-Okar 2001). Nevertheless, the regime promulgated a new political party law in 1992, the effect of which was to restrict the power of the Islamists in parliament. Yet the Islamists remained powerful; even when they decided to boycott the 1997 elections, prominent independent Islamists ran for election and were able to win seats in parliament (Lust-Okar 2001).

By 2003, the opposition had returned to parliament, with many struggles against the regime, mainly concerning electoral reform. They demanded the abolition of the one person, one vote system and called for the redrawing of electoral districts. However, the regime did not respond to any of these demands and continued using the same laws. The regime was determined to undermine Islamists, especially after the success of Hamas in Palestine during the 2006 elections, and in light of Al Qaeda's growing power (al-Qady 2015). This parliament, however, had only six Islamist members out of 110. Yet the regime dismissed the parliament two years before it had completed its term (Ryan 2018). A split between those who want to participate in elections and those who want to boycott ensued, dividing the movement, both leaders and members. In 2007 this polarization and split within the movement had come to the fore, and internal splits and disputes increased further through 2010 (Brown 2012).

In 2015, a new law was issued to further restrict the power of political parties via a stipulation that parties should have more than 500 individual members who come from at least five different governorates. There was a grace period for compliance with the law; however, this law was a blow to the majority of parties, and as a result, the total number of parties dropped to 14. The law created more challenges for the already weak political parties, and hence they failed to influence public policies and their public support has been scant (Bani Salameh 2017).

The members of political parties the research team reached out to contend that the role of parties in bringing about political change is minimal. Even their presence in parliament does not bode many changes. One member of a leftist political party said that she was elected to parliament in 2003 but due to her political ideas and challenges to the regime, she lost her candidacy in the next parliamentary elections. She believes that her loss was not due to losing her constituency as much as to the security meddling with elections.[3] Other party members argued that the regime deliberately weakens political parties through different means. Another problem is the fact that political

---

[3] Interview, October 2018.

parties are not free to discuss their platforms anywhere, even on university campuses. Although they receive 50,000 Jordanian dinars per annum from the state, this is not enough to help support their platforms or to develop political campaigns. 'The state should endorse political parties, since political parties are the ones that organize political life. The problem, however, is that the state wants us to remain weak'.[4]

The Impact of Concessions on Participation

The 1989 demonstrations, together with the discussions on the National Charter, opened up a political opportunity for various groups, ranging from leftists to conservatives to Islamists, to establish some alliances for further negotiations and to push the boundaries for societal liberalization and change (Ryan 2018). In addition, the 1994 peace treaty with Israel developed a political opportunity for contestation, coalition-building and networking among opposition groups, although it also provoked the regime into making political threats, and it soon began to autocratize and roll back many of the liberalization measures. The peace treaty was highly contested among the public, with much outrage and many demonstrations. Opposition parties also started to work more closely together and to network for the next elections. A result of these street politics was another political closure and new restrictions on freedoms. New laws limiting freedom of speech were enacted, a new electoral law was passed, and the updated press law of 1998 imposed heavy restrictions and fines on the independent press (Salameh 2017). These restrictions took different forms, such as increasing the capital requirements twentyfold, in addition to creating a list of security concerns, and issues that were 'untouchable' by any media outlets (Schwedler 2006). These events were not taken lightly by civil society actors and the opposition, and demonstrations were held against the new press law. In one such demonstration in 1997, nearly a hundred journalists demonstrated outside the prime minister's office. More than fifty of them were arrested and many cameras were damaged, even those belonging to international television crews. This 'marked the beginning of a long series of protest activities as the elections approached' (Schwedler 2003). A few months later, a coalition was formed around two former prime ministers, a few leftist parties, and the Islamic Action Front to boycott the elections (Schwedler 2003). Restrictions were also imposed on demonstrations via changes to the public gatherings law, which limited public protest

---

[4] Interview, November 2018.

organizations (Schwedler 2012). These developments increased the power of professional organizations, which have become important forums for the expression of political dissent. In particular, the associations representing engineers, lawyers, doctors, and pharmacists have been able to use their positions as professional organizations to host different political representations, from Islamists, to leftists, to Arab nationalists. They have voiced their opinions and expressed their opposition to some regime policies, especially peace with Israel (Schwedler 2003).

When King Abdullah II assumed power in 1999 after King Hussein's death, he promised to advance economic and political liberalization. His ascendance to power was smooth, even though King Hussein had abruptly changed the succession from his brother Hassan to his son Abdullah shortly before his death. Abdullah relied heavily on his father's advisers, especially the head of the security services (the *mukhabarat*), demonstrating a commitment to regime continuity rather than rupture (Lucas 2005). He drew back from repression and coercion, and even from harsh crackdowns. He restricted pluralism, while 'naked repression is rare' (Yom 2009, 152). Abdullah's relations with the opposition and with the political elite he inherited from his father demonstrates that in authoritarian regimes where the lines of succession are clear and established, the turnover of new rulers is stable and can result in new 'strategies of control' rather than democratization processes (Yom 2009, 152). The regime did not reduce individual rights, but instead has advanced certain rights while restricting others. Rhetoric on the importance of the rule of law and good governance has increased, while the securitization of the state has also increased. A process of neoliberalization developed whereby in order to implement all its economic reforms, the regime was forced to increase security on the streets to contain public dissent (Schwedler 2012).

The liberalization that was promised by King Abdullah was mainly economic, while political liberalization stalled. He developed strong relations with the Gulf monarchies, which opened the Gulf labour market to Jordanians. He renewed the economic liberalization programme with the International Monetary Fund (IMF) and revived a rapid economic privatization process which had stalled in the preceding decade (Salameh 2017). Autocratization measures were accelerated after the 9/11 World Trade Centre attacks, the rise of political Islam, and the subsequent American-led war against terrorism, followed by the American-led invasion of Iraq in 2003 and the terrorist attacks in Jordan in 2005. In the same period, the Jordanian parliament of 2001 was suspended, and all subsequent parliamentary elections were marred by fraud and regime manipulation (Salameh 2017). In addition, political parties have been targeted by different laws to hamper their ability to win parliamentary seats. Independent civil society organizations and opposition political parties have been publicly condemned for having contacts with both regional and international opposition groups (Schwedler 2012). An important consequence of this is that many civil society actors have decided to refrain from accepting funds from international donors. One informant, for instance, said that 'I do not accept foreign funding, because the issues I am active in are too sensitive [politically]. This makes my job very hard, as I do not receive foreign funds, yet Jordanian citizens, in addition to the Jordanian private sector, do not want to fund politically sensitive issues'.[5]

The Uprisings of 2011 and the Changing Political Context

As in most Arab states, demonstrations took place in Jordan during the wave of Arab uprisings in 2010–2011. These demonstrations did not attract many protesters; the largest, in February 2011, mobilized almost 10,000 people. Their demands fluctuated from wanting the parliament (not the king) to elect the prime minister to changing the electoral law (al-Qady 2015). Violence was rare, and only one protester died during clashes with the police. The king reacted quickly, changing a few laws, establishing a national dialogue committee to propose constitutional amendments, and rolling back the structural adjustment and economic liberalization that had been initiated so far. By the end of 2012, however, when the regime lifted some subsidies to rein in the budget deficit, large-scale demonstrations erupted. Activists mobilized throughout the whole country, not only in Amman (Beck and Hüser 2015). Demonstrations also erupted in the East Bank, where the tribes had traditionally aligned with the king. The protests were diverse, ranging from the March 24 Youth movement to the Brotherhood, to the East Jordanians in Karak and Tafileh. During this time, the Hirak, or popular mobilization movement, formed around young East Jordanian activists who supported the Brotherhood. They called for an end to corruption and for a reform of economic and political institutions (Beck and Hüser 2015, 87). From 2011 to 2014, more than 15,000 contentious events took place. They varied in their demands, some calling for socioeconomic reforms and some for political reforms (al-Qady 2015). While the number and scope of the Hirak has increased since the Arab Uprisings of 2011, their general outlook has been more accommodating to the regime, with a large acceptance of the legitimacy of the Hashemite Kingdom. According to al-Majaly

[5] Interview, October 2018.

(2015) both the regime and protest movement actors have agreed throughout the past few years, that peaceful demonstrations and non-violence by both the regime and movements are important in advancing policy reforms.

These quick policy concessions created several political opportunities for the opposition. For instance, constitutional amendments were introduced, such as the establishment of an Independent Elections Commission (IEC) to supervise elections (Bani Salameh 2017; al-Qady 2015). Later, in 2016, the government presented a new electoral law to 'strengthen issue-based political parties in Jordan and move toward the king's stated goal of coalescing Jordan's 50 or so small parties into a few major political parties' (Karmel and Linfeld 2021). The Islamic Action Front (the political wing of the Muslim Brotherhood) was the first party to register under this law (Brown 2012). Although the regime initially responded to the demonstrations with rapid policy changes and a low level of repression, it was soon to pass restrictive laws that would legally protect its repressive actions and deter activists from further dissent activities (Josua and Edel 2021).

Concessions after the Arab Uprisings

The presence of large numbers of activists on the streets of Jordan during the past decade and their ability to mobilize have been the result of the political opportunities that have arisen since the Arab uprisings of 2010–2011. The Hirak movement was important in contentious politics, since new movements and groups emerged as a result, including activists who had been in the opposition in the past decades, as well as new activists. Many of these activists were members of tribes in the East Bank, but Jordanians from Palestinian backgrounds also took part in the Hirak (Schwedler 2022). The regime has tolerated a low level of demonstrations, permitting contention and mobilization within certain red lines, but this subdued level is also the result of its soft and targeted repressive strategies. Within these red lines, activists have been able to demand policy and other changes and to call for mobilization. This activity has also been made possible because the majority of activists are demanding specific social, economic, and political reforms, rather than an overhaul of the system. They focused mainly on their social and economic grievances, criticizing their tribal elders, and the increase in corruption across the country (Schwedler 2022). In our sample, for instance, only one interviewee wanted a total reform of the system. 'We do not want total change, but we want political reform on the national level. We started in 2012, after the Arab uprisings, but unfortunately since then we have not seen real change, except for the Hirak that was developed by young people in different areas of the country.'[6] Another activist argued that 'I am not against the state or the regime; I am actually in favor of the regime. I am politically active for the sake of Jordan. I do not want regime change. People in the Hirak do not want regime change, we want people to be mobilized only to advance reforms'.[7]

Decades of political and economic liberalization and dependence on World Bank and IMF conditionalities have led to economic austerity measures, but also to a rise in corruption. Some activists believe that the austerity measures have weakened state institutions, as well as the political elite's ability to advance economic reforms that differ from those promoted by the international financial institutions:

> The demand of the political, social, and youth movements in Jordan is to bring the state institutions back to the forefront of the country's leadership goals. The privatization process that has been going on has marginalized Jordanian citizens, and the traditional Jordanian political elite was also marginalized in this process. We also call for reform of the political system.[8]

Another interviewee commented that, 'When there is a parliament that does not represent the people, all the while parliamentarians do not address or ask for their citizens' needs, then citizens need to take matters in their own hands … now citizens like me and you are the victims of the government's and the parliament's policies'.[9] Another interviewee argued that, 'The main goal is not to stop taxation, but to send a clear message to the government and policy makers that the people want to defend themselves. The parliament does not represent me and does not represent a lot of people. The unions and syndicates are more important, and they have a big impact on networking and mobilization'.[10]

One activist asserted that:

> In 2011 we started out as a 'labour' demand movement in XX. We need employment, and we suffer from marginalization, unemployment, and poverty. The Hirak here started independently, but then we started to organize ourselves. Then we started developing a committee, and we have a general secretary who foresees

---

[6] Focus group, November 2018.
[7] Focus group, November 2018.
[8] Interview, November 2018.
[9] Interview, July 2018.
[10] Interview, July 2018.

our demands. At the start our demands were purely economic, but then they started developing into demands for political change and calls for a constitutional democracy.[11]

Nevertheless, there is an important distinction between activists who live in Amman and those living in tribal areas. Activists in Amman direct their demands for reform to the government, but in tribal areas and in the governorates, they ask the king directly.[12] After the 2011 uprisings, different opposition groups developed their own protest movements, with a large number originating in the East Bank and in different governorates rather than in Amman (see, for instance, Ryan 2018 and Schwedler 2006, 2022). Mobilization is another important strategy of the East Bankers, who had hitherto been the backbone of the regime. In some areas like Madaba and Dhiban, services are poor, and the citizens feel that they

> … did not receive a fair share of development like other areas in the country. We feel that we are unfairly treated. We called for demonstrations in 2011 to have more social protections and socioeconomic development. Since then, we have established Hirak Dhiban and developed different committees to ensure that our mobilization continues to pressure the regime. When the regime did not do anything, however, the majority of citizens here boycotted the parliamentary elections [in 2016]. During the following elections one of the activists in the Hirak contested and won a parliamentary seat. People here had very high trust levels toward the Hirak activists, unlike the government and the parliamentarians. The [outcome of the] contest [was] winning the parliamentary seat.[13]

By 2013, some observers believed that the Hirak was over, since many of its participants had been co-opted by the regime, and coercion had also closed down the opportunity for more activism (Ryan 2018). Another major contentious episode occurred in 2018, when demonstrations erupted spontaneously in response to a proposed income tax law, which resulted in the ouster of Prime Minister Hani Mulki's government a week after the demonstrations began. It was an example of how collective challenges to authority emerge when broad socioeconomic developments open up political opportunities by unsettling the existing power relations and/or by increasing the leverage of marginalized populations (McAdam 1982). 'Excluded groups

---

[11] Interview, July 2018.
[12] Interview, July 2018.
[13] Interview, July 2018.

mobilize by using pre-existing organizations and networks to recruit members and appropriating elements of culture and ideas to frame their visions in ways to animate support' (McAdam et al.1996).

The Fourth Circle Demonstrations

In 2018, thousands of Jordanians took to the streets in almost every city, in some of the biggest demonstrations in years. The protesters rejected the new proposed income tax law, as well as the latest price hikes on fuel derivatives and electricity and called for Prime Minister Hani Mulki to be dismissed. According to Darwish (2018), '[w]hile protests did not receive enough coverage by local media in Jordan, social media platforms seemed to carry the weight of conveying what is happening on the ground'. On June 5, 2018, the prime minister was dismissed, and the king ordered the government to suspend the increases in energy prices (Sweis 2018).

This event illustrates some important dynamics of contention in Jordan, and points to the larger picture, namely that the political context provided an opportunity for mass demonstrations to take place. How did the mobilization for this event occur, and what were the underlying grievances of the activists who participated in it? Is mobilization a result of previously established networks, or were these networks just spontaneous protests that faded once the prime minister was removed?

This time the mobilization was sparked by the trade unions, who chose the Fourth Circle in Amman as the meeting point for the sit-in during the month of Ramadan, at the end of May 2018.[14] The Fourth Circle is Amman's major roundabout, where the parliament, government buildings, and embassies are located. The mobilization travelled quickly to other governorates, with 'more than 40 points of demonstrations'.[15] The choice of the space in which demonstrations took place was critical (Schwedler 2022).

> The geographical place of the Fourth Circle is very important, because it is a live area in the kingdom. Demonstrations in al Salt for instance were not as influential as the ones in the Fourth Circle .... One of the reasons why the sit-in was successful during this time is because they did not have any involvement from political parties. As long as the goal was one, we were able to attain it.[16]

---

[14] Interview, July 2018.
[15] Interview, June 2018.
[16] Interview, June 2018.

Space is analysed in social movement studies as a means of facilitating further mobilization of networks and to demonstrate grievances. Spatial environments create various repertoires of contention and can become important tools for activists' contentious repertoires (Salmenkari 2009).

Activists were adamant about bringing people onto the streets, since a large majority of activists believe that street mobilization for socioeconomic or issue-oriented reform can only be achieved through street contention.

> For us, demonstrations are the only solution to our problems, since the Jordanian street is the only way through which we can push for change and it is the only one possible to push the regime for reform. We were able to walk in different demonstrations [and] we conducted a few strikes and sit-ins in different governorates, and in Amman. We made many statements where we showed that our main goal is that we need drastic reforms, reaching the abolition of the king's power, transparent popular participation, and democracy.[17]

Even though street contention is essential for reversing unfavourable policies, many activists referred to the importance of social networking sites, especially Twitter. According to one interviewee's account, 'The mobilization process started on Twitter and Facebook, mainly Twitter, but during the sit-in, the activists themselves would discuss how to continue the sit-in. However, the coordination was not very effective, and this is mainly due to the activists' lack of political experience'.[18]

Another interviewee argued that the demonstrations were abrupt and contingent, and the unions' sit-in and strike were very important because they brought new people to demonstrate.

There were a few groups who would have never participated before.[19] According to an interviewee, there were no major coalition partnerships between activists. Mobilization was created mainly through social networking sites. Some Facebook pages, for instance, mobilized for the demonstrations, but it was mainly the activists at the Fourth Circle who decided together that they would return the next day to continue the sit-in.[20] In XX village, activists called for meetings during the Fourth Circle demonstration. More than 200 people participated in these meetings, and the majority were in favour of the Hirak.[21]

---

[17] Ibid.
[18] Interview, June 2018.
[19] Interview, June 2018.
[20] Interview, June 2018.
[21] Focus group, November 2018.

Mobilization in other cities, however, faced some challenges. One interviewer gave an account of events:

> Mobilization is not an easy task in tribal areas. For instance, during the Fourth Circle demonstrations, people used to come to al-Huriya square and find seventy to a hundred people. Jerash has a large population, so this is not logical. Why? They say they want security and safety ... [and] because the tribes give a sense of security, people are hesitant to be mobilized with the Hirak.[22]

Networking between different movements and activists has taken place, although it has not often been deep. 'Throughout the years we built different coalitions, like XX coalition and XX coalition, which included twelve different movements'.[23]

Hence, the call for demonstrations and sit-ins by the trade unions was important for mobilizing many people, because of the unions' large memberships in all governorates. One of the major slogans of the demonstrations was '*ma'anash*' ['We do not have'], referring to the rising poverty in Jordan, which leaves many people unable to afford the higher taxes (al-Shara'an 2019).

Field Opportunity Structures and Targeted Repression

The field opportunity structure is in the non-state sphere, where different social actors sometimes help and at other times constrain activism. In many authoritarian contexts, activism, movements, mobilization, and contestation have been demonized by incumbent dictators in different ways. Media campaigns depicting the civil war in Syria and the repressive events in Egypt from the perspective of the regimes have taken a toll on how many in those societies perceive activists. For instance, some activists in our sample described experiencing social and family pressures critical of their activism. According to one interviewee:

> I am *persona non grata* in society. I did a show on TV and uploaded it on Facebook,[24] and I received a lot of criticism. Like, why do you talk in our name, who are you? One person said that 'I respect you, but with your mobilization on the street you are now an outcast in society and people now hate you' ... so people dislike me as an activist on the street ... I swear we do not want to destroy

---

[22] Interview, August 2018.
[23] Focus group, November 2018.
[24] The show mainly highlighted corruption and economic problems in Jordan.

the country. On the contrary we are pro the Hashemite family; me and all other movements want to reform the economic, social, and political process. There is no need for corruption or favouritism in the public sector. We want reform, not change.[25]

Another activist in a tribal village in the southern part of the country explained that:

> The Hirak to which my group belongs is called *XX*. However, when we first started, our community was against us, and they believed that we were working to destroy the state. However, what we have demanded in terms of anti-corruption measures, for instance, has been taken into consideration by the regime. The regime established the organization to stop corruption and the *diwan al-muhassaba* [audit diwan]. However, these were only a sort of painkiller, so that people could see there is a will to end corruption.[26]

Another activist contended that, 'Repression by the regime is not high; however, sometimes parents prevent their daughters from going to the demonstrations. Facebook had a positive influence as well, because during the demonstrations and sit-ins young people used to "go live" so they would bring more public attention to their cause'.[27] Some women activists, however, have argued that they have at times defied their parents to continue their activism. For instance, one said that 'My family does not support me. Now I am angry to the extent that I do not care if my parents are afraid and just want to protect me. During the Fourth Circle demonstrations I used to go without their consent. I actually did not tell them that I was going to demonstrate'.[28]

> The context here is interesting, because there is 'ebb and flow when it comes to trust between movements and citizens at large. Sometimes there are high trust levels and at others no trust at all'. In XX for instance, my friends and I started a small movement. We started with a 'silent movement' where we had placards where we would write reform measures we wanted, especially changing the economic status of Jordan … at the start we had very few members; my friends and I were no more than ten people. When citizens would come out of the mosque after prayers, they would be angry with us …. However, in Ramadan the Fourth Circle demonstrations

---

[25] Interview, August 2018.
[26] Focus group, November 2018.
[27] Interview, July 2018.
[28] Interview, November 2018.

were important, because the Hirak made people understand how the political and economic are related.[29]

Targeted Repression and Its Discontents: Internal Splits

According to thirteen interviewees in our sample of fifty-three, internal splits and ideological divergences among activists are the main causes of their weakness. Another ten believed that an inability to mobilize others to their cause is the major reason for their weakness.

> We also established a platform called *taqadom* [progress] where we networked with different human rights and democracy advocates in Jordan. We wanted to establish a third tier, without the Muslim Brotherhood and without pro-regime organizations or parties. We wanted to bring in people together who believe in the basic ideas of a democratic, civil state and an economy based on industrialization and personal freedoms. Nevertheless, after 2013, I left because the activists did not find solutions, but only wanted to mobilize others to the street.[30]

Another activist said, 'When young people from the governorates joined the demonstrations, their slogans and demands were much higher than the activists in Amman, so youth from the Fourth Circle were afraid; our demands are different than those from the governorates, because our living standards are totally different. They feel marginalized by the state, and we feel marginalized economically'.[31] While union members had one major demand—to stop the proposed income tax law—other activists who joined the demonstrations and sit-in had different demands. The spaces in which the sit-in would take place were clear from the start, and the date was also already decided. Thus they were hesitant to support more demands.[32]

The regime utilizes several methods of repression to weaken activists and their movements. In one form or another, repression is believed to be the major cause of weakness in the movements, and also of activists deciding to disengage. An important aspect in the strategies of repression is the fact that East Bank Jordanians are the most vocal in their contentious activities and

---

[29] Interview, October 2018.
[30] Interview, June 2018.
[31] Interview, August 2018.
[32] Interview, June 2018.

criticism of the regime, yet they are also the dominant force in the security apparatus (Schwedler 2022). This is a double-edged sword, since the security apparatus can use different strategies of control on activists who belong to the same tribes as members of the security forces, for example playing on shared tribal affiliations for sympathy.

During the past two decades, the neoliberalization process taking place in Jordan has impacted protest spatiality. The different infrastructural projects and the new urban developments have created some possibilities for continuous activities, yet they have also made the spaces for demonstrations more visible, and hence some spaces are 'more exposed and visible for surveillance' (Schwedler 2022, 25). According to thirty-six activists in our sample, repression is on the rise in Jordan, and it is the main reason for people not joining their movements and for their own families and friends encouraging them to stop participating in activism. Many activists argued that since the events in Egypt of 2013 and the escalating civil war in Syria, the regime in Jordan has amped up its repressive strategies against activists and movements. It also uses its machine to frighten people away from joining activists and movements. 'The authorities have used what is happening elsewhere in the region to scare citizens off. They show what happened in Syria and implicitly threaten that it could happen in Jordan if people join our movements. Those citizens that are risk averse do not want to go to the street, and the regime uses a discourse that demonizes activists'.[33] Others argue that the regime in Jordan is better than those in Egypt and Syria: 'The security is not great, but the regime is cleverer than others in the region. They do not use much physical force; some people can be imprisoned, but it is not that bad. I was never even beaten by the police during any of the demonstrations in which I participated'.[34]

The regime's repressive measures range from media campaigns against activists to the use of physical force. Even though these repressive measures can be seen as widespread repressive policies, when analysed further it is clear that the use of targeted repression is more pervasive. Activists argue, for instance, that laws have been passed during the last few years restricting freedoms and political participation. They regard the cybersecurity law as the root cause of reduced mobilization. Even though the law had not yet been ratified when the fieldwork for this research took place, it was part of the 2018 national cybersecurity strategy which was enacted by the regime.

---

[33] Interview, November 2018.
[34] Interview, November 2018.

This law (No. 16/2019) was promulgated in 2019 and has been essential for cracking down on activists and limiting freedoms.[35]

There has also been increasing restrictions on reporters since 2015, with some forced to stop work because they had published anti-regime rhetoric. Self-censorship is a major issue for some activists. 'I know that there is corruption in Jordan and that there are citizens above the law, and I know that these people have impunity, but I don't talk about it. It is self-censorship. Also, when I talk about gender issues and sexuality, I do not talk freely.'[36]

More importantly, the regime uses targeted and subtle repressive measures. An activist who participated in the Fourth Circle demonstrations explained that 'the security services called on some activists who mobilized for the sit-in; however, they did not call upon them during the sit-in, only afterward. They were also only held for a few hours. No one was detained.'[37] One activist observed that 'the security personnel deal differently with demonstrators. When there are a lot of cameras and media, they are lenient. However, once the media and large numbers of demonstrators leave, the security personnel start intimidating people. They use verbal harassment and sometimes they hit people. I myself was hit in the Fourth Circle and my friend was also hit in front of me.'[38] Another said, 'I can't work in any job which requires security permissions, since I have been imprisoned seven times since 2011. I can travel and go back and forth, but job opportunities are very scarce for me.'[39] Others have argued that security personnel use subtle threats to frighten people away from joining demonstrations. They call activists to threaten that if they continue their activism, their family members will lose their jobs, for instance.[40]

As mentioned previously, the dynamics of mobilization are different for those from the East and tribal areas compared to those from Amman:

> Ammani citizens are mostly from the West Bank and are afraid to protest or to go against the regime. They fear that the regime might deny them their residency or harm them. They are not backed or protected by a tribe. We in the governorates and East Bankers, on the other hand, are not afraid. The regime cannot revoke our residency. Even when the regime decides to crack down on me, or detain me, I

---

[35] For more information on the law see, for instance, Sevan Araz. 2023. 'Jordan adopts sweeping cybersecurity legislation'. *Middle East Institute*, online at: https://www.mei.edu/publications/jordan-adopts-sweeping-cybersecurity-legislation; retrieved 9 January.
[36] Interview, December 2018.
[37] Interview, June 2018.
[38] Interview, July 2018.
[39] Interview, July 2018.
[40] Interview, November 2018.

have hundreds of people backing me who will demonstrate and mobilize for my release.[41]

Another activist commented that, 'People who were active in Hirak Jerash lost their jobs.'[42]

According to an interviewee who participated in the 2012 demonstrations, 'We are now very weak. Due to security pressures, the majority of us have either changed our political beliefs or have left the country.'[43] Another interviewee explained that:

> Our work and mobilizational abilities are dependent on the political context, and the time and space in which we work. For instance, there are many movements in XX [in the East Bank] but they are all dependent on the political context. At times there have been many political and security constraints. For instance, before the Fourth Circle demonstrations, we used to see a lot of security harassment of activists, and it impacted freedom of speech; we used to work on various issues, and we had many constraints from the security. However, after *habbet* Ramadan [the Fourth Circle demonstrations], thank God we can go to the streets on a daily basis and people can call for their demands in a peaceful manner, and the security do not harass them. We actually have had positive relations with the security. However, during the past few years I have been a member of XX. I am the media spokesperson for this movement and have been called upon by the *mukhabarat* during the past week along with other activists, because we have been calling for more street demonstrations. So we are now facing new closure and constraints on political activists.[44]

Smear campaigns are also devised against activists. For instance, an activist in the teachers' union argues that 'We were not able to mobilize as much as we could because the *mukhabarat* was working against us. In addition, newspapers, mainly *al-Ra'y* and some other electronic news outlets which have direct relations with the security services, have done counter revolutionary work and smear campaigns against us.'[45] Activists asserted that the media is full of state propaganda against them that claims that activists want to destroy the state.[46] The state security personnel have authority to choose individuals for high public positions in the governorates, like Ma'an, for instance, so

---

[41] Interview, July 2018.
[42] Interview, August 2018.
[43] Interview, June 2018.
[44] Interview, September 2018.
[45] Interview, August 2018.
[46] Interview, November 2018.

only those who have shown acceptable levels of loyalty and obedience will be rewarded with powerful jobs.[47]

Co-optation measures are also utilized, and when activists resist these, they are repressed. For instance, one activist from the East Bank who mobilized for the Fourth Circle demonstrations said that 'Security and government officials have reached out to me to stop my mobilizational strategies and activism through providing me with prominent job opportunities. They also have promised to find employment opportunities for my family members as well'.[48]

The regime's repressive strategies towards activists have some similarities with that of the Egyptian regime, especially concerning the smear campaigns and threats against activists and their families. Nevertheless, the regime in this case does not resort to physical violence like the Egyptian regime. Even activists who are 'politically' engaged and who mobilize for large-scale demonstrations against the regime are rarely subjected to physical violence or imprisonment, as in Egypt. The Jordanian regime's strategies of repression and concessions towards these activists is more similar to that of the Mubarak regime from the 1990s until his ouster. This demonstrates how long-standing authoritarian regimes utilize more targeted repression and more concessions than those undergoing authoritarian regime-building.

Conclusion

In the previous discussion I have shown how the Black September event of 1970 impacted the political context in Jordan and the regime's subsequent strategies towards political opposition, activists, and movements. The regime uses targeted repression mainly against those activists who mobilize in the street to protest its policies. At the same time, the regime relies heavily on the co-optation of different tribes and social actors, in addition to making concessions in the form of political liberalization. Activists are well aware of the red lines which constrain them and are careful to mobilize for change within these boundaries. Intermittent use of targeted repression and co-optation has sometimes opened up political opportunities for activists to mobilize for demonstrations at certain critical junctures. These same strategies are, however, sometimes utilized as a political threat to demobilize the public. Hence, during protest events such as the 2018 Fourth Circle contention, targeted repression against certain leading activists, in addition to the co-option of others, led to demobilization—and concessions from the regime sometimes

---
[47] Ibid.
[48] Interview, November 2018.

had the same result. Unlike in Egypt, the regime utilizes targeted and subtle repression towards activists, mainly those who have the capability to mobilize people to take to the streets. These strategies, have proven effective in containing large-scale demonstrations and advancing demobilization, without the resort to diffuse repression.

Bibliography

al-Majaly, Abd al-Salam. 2003. *re'hlet al-'umr: min bayt al-shi'ir ila sadato al-hukm [Life Journey]*. Beirut: All Prints Distributors and Publishers.

al-Majaly, Radwan Mahmoud. 2015. '"athar al-harakat al-'ihtijajiyya fy al-urdun" ala al-istiqrar al-siyassy [The Impact of the Protst Movements in Jordan on Political Stability]'. *Dafatir al-siyassa wa-al-Qanun* (12): 49–64.

al-Manaseer, Mohamed. 2011. *Ammon News*. 9 May. Accessed 20 February 2023. https://www.ammonnews.net/article/96403.

al-Qady, Adel T. 2015. 'al-ihtijajat al-sha'abiyya wa al-isslah al-siyassi fy al-urdun: (2011–2014) [Public demonstrations and political reform in Jordan: 2011–2014]'. *al-manara* 21 (3): 73–113.

al-Shara'an, Mahmoud. 2019. 'hirak al-urdun … lematha yataghayyar saqf al-shi'arat wa al-madaleb? [The Jordanian Hirak … Why the change in the slogan's and demands' ceilings?]' *Al Jazeera*. 9 February. Accessed 21 December 2021. https://www.aljazeera.net/news/politics/2019/2/9/%D8%A3%D8%B1%D8%AF%D9%86-%D8%AD%D8%B1%D8%A7%D9%83-%D8%B4%D8%B9%D8%A7%D8%B1%D8%A7%D8%AA-%D9%87D8%AA%D8%A7%D9%81-%D9%85%D8%B7%D8%A7%D9%84%D8%A8-%D8%A7%D9%84%D8%B9%D8%A7%D8%B5%D9%85%D8%A9.

Ancelovici, Marcos. 2021. 'Bourdieu in movement: Toward a field theory of contentious politics'. *Social Movement Studies* 20 (2): 155–173.

Ancelovici, Marcos. 2021. 'Conceptualizing the context of collective action: an introduction'. *Social Movement Studies* 20 (2): 125–138.

Azzam, Majid Abu. 2020. 'Munazamaat al-mujtama' al-madany al-murtabita b-hokuk al-mar'a wa 'ilaqatha ma' al-hokuma fy al-urdun [Civil society organizations that are linked with women's rights and its relations with the Jordanian government]'. *Al-Dimuqratiyya*, 53–58.

Bani Salameh, Mohamed. 2017. 'Political reform in Jordan: Reality and aspirations'. *World Affairs Journal* 180 (4). https://doi.org/10.1177/0043820018765373

Beck, Martin and Simone Hüser. 2015. 'Jordan and the 'Arab Spring': No challenge, no change?' *Middle East Critique* 24 (1): 83–97.

Benstead, Lindsay. 2016. 'Conceptualizing and measuring patriarchy: The importance of feminist theory'. *POMEPS Studies* (May) 19: 8–12.

Bishara, Dina. 2014. 'Labor Movements in Tuisia and Egypt: Drivers vs. Objects of Change in Transition from Authoritarian Rule'. https://www.swp-berlin.org/fileadmin/contents/products/comments/2014C01_bishara.pdf.

Brand, Laurie. 1994. *Jordan's Inter-Arab Relations: The Political Economy of Alliance Making*. New York: Columbia University Press.

Brown, Nathan. 2012. *When Victory Is not an Option: Islamist Movements in Arab Politics*. Ithaca, NY: Cornell University Press.

Cavatorta, Francesco and Janine A. Clark. 2022. 'Political and social mobilization in the Middle East and North Africa after the 2011 uprisings'. *Globalizations* 1–15 DOI: 10.1080/14747731.2021.2012910.

Clark, Janine. 2012. 'Patronage, presitge, and power: The Islamic center charity societys political role within the Muslim Brotherhood'. In *Islamist Politics in the Middle East: Movements and Change*, by Samer Shehata, 68–88. London: Routledge.

Clark, Janine. 2018. *Local Politics in Jordan and Morocco: Strategies of Centralization and Decentralization*. New York: Columbia University Press.

Conrad, Courtenay. 2011. 'Constrained concessions: Beneficent dictatorial responses to the domestic political opposition'. *International Studies Quarterly* 55 (4): 1167–1187.

Darwish, Randa. 2018. 'Jordanian protests grab headlines for the fourth consecutive day'. *Al Bawaba: Your Gateway to the Middle East*. 3 June. Accessed 13 December 2021. https://www.albawaba.com/loop/jordanian-protests-grab-headlines-fourth-consecutive-day-1140718.

Davenport, Christian. 2009. 'Regimes, repertoires and state repression'. *Swiss Political Science Review* 15 (2): 377–385.

Della Porta, Donatella and Mario Diani. 2006. *Social Movements: An Introduction*, 2nd edn. Malden: Blackwell Publishing.

Ellen Lust-Okar. 2001. 'The decline of Jordanian political parties: Myth or reality?' *International Journal of Middle East Studies* 33 (4): 545–569 DOI: https://doi.org/10.1017/S0020743801004044

Falleti, Tulia G and Julia F Lynch. 2009. 'Context and causal mechanisms in political analysis'. *Comparative Political Studies* 42 (9): 1143–1166.

Gallets, Barbara. 2015. 'Black september and identity constructionin Jordan'. *Journal of Georgetown University-Qatar MIddle Eastern Studies Student Association* (1): https://doi.org/10.5339/messa.2015.12.

Goldstone, Jack and Charles Tilly. 2001. 'Threat (and opportunity): Popular action and state response in the dynamics of contentious action'. In *Silence and Voice in the Study of Contentious Politics*, by Ronald Aminzade, 179–194. Cambridge: Cambridge University Press.

Hildebrandt, Timothy. 2013. *Social Origins of the Authoritarian State in China*. Cambridge: Cambridge University Press.

Husseini, Rana. 2017. 'In historic vote, house abolishes controversial Article 308'. *The Jordan Times*. 1 August. Accessed December 2021. https://www.jordantimes.com/news/local/historic-vote-house-abolishes-controversial-article-308.

Josua, Maria and Mirjam Edel. 2021. 'The Arab uprisings and the return of repression'. *Mediterranean Politics* 26 (5): 586–611.

Karmel, EJ and David Linfeld. 2021. 'Jordan's election law: Reinforcing barriers to democracy'. *Middle East Law and Governance* 13 (3): 1–14. https://doi.org/10.1163/18763375-13031307.

Khusa, Amad Abu. 1991. *al-Dimuqratiyya wa al-ahzab al-siyassiyya al-urduniyya [Democracy and Political Parties in Jordan]*. Amman: Middle East Publishing Company.

Köprülü, Nur. 2017. 'Electoral pluralism, social division and the 2016 parliamentary elections in Jordan'. *Digest of Middle East Studies* 26 (2): 278–298.

Lucas, Russel. 2005. *Institutions and the Politics of Survival in Jordan: Domestic Responses to External Challenges, 1988–2001*. New York: The State University of New York Press.

Lucas, Russell. 2008. 'Side effects of regime building in Jordan: The state and the nation'. *Civil Wars* 10 (3): 281–293.

Masaad, Joseph. 2001. *Colonial Effects: The Making of National Identity in Jordan*. New York: Columbia University Press.

McAdam, Doug. 1982. *Political Process and the Development of Black Insurgency: 1930–1970*. Chicago: University of Chicago Press.

McAdam, Doug, John McCarrthy, and Meyer E. Zald. 1996. *Comparative Perspectives on Social Movements: Political Opportunities, Mobilizing Structures and Cultural Framings*. Cambridge: Cambridge University Press.

Moss, Dana. 2014. 'Repression, response, and contained escalation under "liberalized" authoritarianism in Jordan'. *Mobilization* 19 (3): 262–286.

Nevo, Joseph. 2008. 'September 1970 in Jordan: A Civil War?' *Civil Wars* 10 (3): 217–230.

Ryan, Curtis. 2018. *Jordan and the Arab Uprisings: Regime Survival and Politics Beyond the State*. New York: Columbia University Press.

Salameh, Mohammed Torki Bani. 2017. 'Political reform in Jordan'. *World Affairs* 180 (4): 47–78.

Salmenkari, Taru. 2009. 'Geography of protest: Demonstration in Buenos Aires and Seoul'. *Urban Geography* 30 (3): 238–260.

Schwedler, Jillian. 2003. 'More than a mob: The dynamics of political demonstrations in Jordan'. *Middle East Report* (Spring): 18–23.

Schwedler, Jillian. 2006. *Fairth in Moderation: Islamist Parties in Jordan and Yemen.* New York: Cambridge University Press.

Schwedler, Jillian. 2012. 'The political geography of protest in Neoliberal Jordan'. *Middle East Critique* 21 (3): 259–270.

Schwedler, Jillian. 2022. *Protesting Jordan: Geographies of Power and Dissent.* Stanford: Stanford University Press.

Sweis, Rana. 2018. 'Jordan's prime minister quits as protestors demand an end to austerity'. *The New York Times.* 4 June. Accessed 13 December 2021. https://www.nytimes.com/2018/06/04/world/middleeast/jordan-strike-protest.html.

Sydney, Tarrow. 1998. *Power in Movement: Social Movements and Contentious Politics.* New York: Cambridge University Press.

Tarrow, Sydney. 1996. 'Social movements in contentious politics: A review article'. *The American Political Science Review* 90 (4): 874–883

Tilly, Charles and Sidney Tarrow. 2006. *Contentious Politics.* Oxford: Oxford University Press.

UN Women. 2017. *Jordanian Parliament abolishes law that allowed rapists to avoid prosecution by marrying their victims.* 4 August. Accessed 7 December 2021. https://www.unwomen.org/en/news/stories/2017/8/news-jordanian-parliament-abolishes-law-that-allowed-rapists-to-avoid-prosecution.

Volpi, Frédéric and Janine Clark. 2019. 'Activism in the Middle East and North Africa in times of upheaval: Social networks' actions and interactions'. *Social Movement Studies* 18 (1): 1–16.

Yom, Sean. 2009. 'Jordan: Ten more years of autocracy'. *Journal of Democracy* 20 (4): 151–166.

Yuen, Samson and Edmund W. Cheng. 2017. 'Neither repression nor concession? A regime's attrition against mass protests'. *Political Studies* 65 (3): 611–630. https://doi.org/10.1177/0032321716674024

5
Coalition Partnerships in Light of Concessions and Targeted Repression in Jordan

The reliance on concessions in the form of political liberalization processes with authoritarian measures of control, like targeted repression against the opposition, have had an impact on the extent to which civil society actors are able to develop different coalition partnerships and networks in Jordan. These coalitions and networks are important in advancing some social and economic changes and can also exert pressure on the regime to change some policies. Like many other developing countries, in the 1990s and early 2000s Jordan ventured into economic liberalization. At the same time, the government opened up the public sphere for civil society, especially for non-governmental organizations (NGOs). However, to ensure that civil society was constrained, the regime passed laws that were only sufficient to accommodate the international community's endorsement of NGOs for development purposes and to showcase political liberalization of the public sphere. Allowing limited civil and political participation can also help autocratic rulers obtain citizens' feedback on various policies in order to respond quickly to social and economic challenges (Lorch and Bunk 2017). Although the king had dissolved parliament in 2001 and reconvened it only in 2003, he promulgated various laws to prevent street mobilization in support of the Al-Aqsa Intifada (2000–2005) and also to restrict some freedoms (Yom 2009). Nevertheless, these laws also permitted the continuing presence of different civil society actors who were affected by the regime's concession and repression policies. In this chapter I analyse the political context, especially the use of targeted repression towards some activists within movements, and how this impacts coalition-building and networking. Here, targeted repression permits some forms of activism within the confines of regime-permitted red lines. Activism here does not permeate large scale demonstrations, but rather contained demonstrations. As in the previous chapter, I draw on Ancelovici's model, which adds a non-state sphere to the political opportunity structure

Civil Society and Activism in the Middle East. Nadine Sika, Oxford University Press. © Nadine Sika (2024).
DOI: 10.1093/oso/9780198882411.003.0006

in the political process model. This model asserts that society has various fields that encompass different opportunities—the 'field opportunity structure' (Ancelovici 2021). The development of contentious activities can be associated with a change in the structure of the prevailing opportunities. When such an opportunity arises, it increases the capacity of actors to change (Ancelovici 2021; Tarrow 1996, 1998). This puts the state at the centre of the dynamics, which is important for certain civil society actors. For other civil society actors, however, the society at large plays an important role. Hence, civil society actors can target social institutions, which might also influence social, cultural, and political change. Ancelovici (2021, 157) postulates the presence of 'multiple social and institutional spaces within a given society'. For the analysis here, I add both the social and political fields, since society can exert pressure on some movements to keep certain social structures intact, instead of changing them, especially in regard to women's rights and empowerment.

In Jordan, different social actors target different institutions. At times they align with the regime against tribal leaders and conservative forces in society and push for reform and change. However, the regime can then use this alliance against those same actors if/when their activism does not serve its interests. In such a situation, the regime mobilizes society against these same actors to reduce their mobilizational capacity. In the following discussion, I analyse different campaigns that were spearheaded by the women's movement, rather than specific contentious events. The chapter discusses how the authoritarian context in Jordan relies more on concessions than repression when dealing with civil society actors who work in the developmental field, and how these actors utilize the prevalent political and field opportunities to develop coalitions and networks advancing change. This chapter also highlights how targeted repression can be seen as an opportunity by civil society actors to advance certain campaigns, while it also simultaneously diffuses large-scale demonstrations.

Economic Reforms for Social Control

By the early 2000s, the Jordanian regime had enacted new laws favouring privatization and free trade as a prelude to embarking on economic liberalization. These reforms were developed in consultation with international financial institutions, mainly the International Monetary Fund (IMF) and the World Bank. Jordan also became a member of the World Trade Organization in 2000, which affected local politics. A process of decentralization began, and municipalities were reformed and had their budgets cut (Clark 2012). These processes took place alongside the setting up of the Economic Consultative Council (ECC), an advisory board whose main function was to advance reforms by creating partnerships and dialogue between businessmen and the government. 'Together with the political elite, the private sector members of the ECC became powerful drivers and de facto decision-makers of economic neoliberalism in Jordan' (Isleyen and Kreitmeyr 2021, 249).

In addition, economic rights were formulated, such as the protection of foreign direct investments, consumerism, and private property, while other rights, such as political freedoms, freedom of expression, and rights around public protests, were restricted (Schwedler 2012). Yet it can still be argued that economic reforms have been implemented with minimal physical repression, without the use of force or imprisonment. However, certain legal measures were introduced that have limited overall individual and political rights (Schwedler 2012). The economic reforms have impacted Jordan's social structure, in that they have taken a toll on the traditional partnership between the regime and its core backers, in particular the East Bank tribes.[1] East Bankers have many grievances against the neoliberal project which has been enacted by King Abdullah. In 2002 the regime used repression against demonstrators in Ma'an, which silenced dissent there for a while. However, grievances were still high. The privatization processes undertaken by the regime have increased corruption levels. Many areas in the East Bank were impoverished, while mega projects were underway in tourist resorts and in Amman. The agricultural sector has become distressed, adding to an increase in the unemployment problem and an increase in poverty levels (Schwedler 2022).

The neoliberalization and enhanced role of private businesses in the polity has elevated the role of businessmen over that of the regime's former allies. Citizens in the southern part of the country have argued that the economic reforms have shifted the engine of the economy from the public to the private sector, resulting in a parallel shift in the social and political balance of power (Oudat and Alshboul 2010). In response to these developments, activism and mobilization also increased during the decade that began in 2000. Labour protests increased; for instance, 139 labour protests were documented by the Jordan Labor Watch group in 2010 (Schwedler 2022). During the teachers' strike in 2010, which shut down the majority of local schools, the regime targeted prominent teachers' union activists and forced them into

---

[1] For more discussion on the relationship between the regime and the tribes, see Chapter 4.

early retirement. However, when public mobilization increased in support of these teachers, the decision was changed (Schwedler 2022).

To fend off public discontent, the king developed the 'Jordan First' campaign to justify various political and social decisions. It became general consensus among regime insiders that 'Jordanians only belong to Jordan and their loyalty should only be to the Hashemite' (Schwedler 2003). The campaign was intended to draw attention to the influence of foreign powers on Jordanian society and domestic politics and to counter this through a national consensus based around the 'Jordan First' slogan. Instead of bringing stability, however, it fuelled more discontent, and voices were raised opposing different government policies (Ryan 2004). During the research team's fieldwork, activists, especially those living in the East Bank, criticized these policies, arguing that the privatization measures have caused:

> … state weakness, and increased social, economic, and political problems. When we demonstrate against the regime, it is not because we want to have regime breakdown or regime change, but because we want to bring the power of the state back. We want the state institutions to regain their power, because the economic reform policies have increased the power of the private sector, including international actors, which has had a negative impact on us. The economic reform policies since 1989 are at the root cause of all problems we experience today. … Now we are totally marginalized in the polity.[2]

Concessions to Civil Society as a Form of Control

The regime provides sufficient space for independent civil society actors, tribal leadership, professional associations, voluntary organizations, and Islamist movements to exist. Its representatives listen to their opinions and complaints regularly and sometimes even consult them about social problems. This strategy helps to prevent demonstrations and social unrest. Nevertheless, 'the reins of public and political life remain firmly in the hands of the state' (Harmsen 2008, 102). Thus the regime has the upper hand in determining who has the right to be included in the public sphere and who does not, and in setting out the red lines. It also ensures that the laws and regulations for civil society actors are vague enough to allow government authorities and security personnel sufficient leeway to control the red lines in the way that best suits them. Many activists say that the regime uses these

---

[2] Interview, September 2018.

laws selectively to pre-empt activists from demanding rights that go beyond the regime's red lines. 'Sometimes the regime plays with the interpretations of these laws and how they are implemented, to ensure that it keeps its grip on power.'[3]

In addition, laws restricting NGOs have also become more severe. Foreign funds have been restricted, and members of political parties are not allowed to participate in any international events at which Jordan might be insulted (Schwedler 2012). Thus the regime can ensure that it monitors all political activity. If the media overstep the red lines, or if a peaceful demonstration is considered to be politically sensitive, the state can prevent or pre-empt these by applying different laws. To ensure its survival, the regime continues to communicate with different civil society actors in order to keep in touch with activities at the grassroots. It is therefore open to criticism and suggestions from some organizations or civil society actors— who at the same time take care not to cross certain red lines and to keep the interests of the regime a top priority (Harmsen 2008, 12). These dynamics demonstrate how an authoritarian regime tries both to build consent with and assert hegemony over civil society actors without using excessive physical coercion and repression. It is easier to do this with civil society actors who are primarily interested in advancing modernization and development than with organizations campaigning for human rights and political reform. Many activists to whom the research team reached out are networked in different organizations with a foot in both camps—they move from the human rights sector to the charity sector or work in both fields simultaneously. Many women activists in particular explain that they started their careers in the human rights field, calling for equality and citizenship rights, and then developed their activism towards calling for women's rights and equality. Thus civil society is not 'separate' from political society. However, the regime develops an array of strategies to keep political activism at bay and 'actively deploys' some NGOs and activists to advance changes that serve its interests (see, for instance, Alagappa 2004; Grevaso and Teti 2021; Chalcraft 2021).

> The state cooperates a lot and helps us when we talk about women's empowerment. However, when we call for freedoms and human rights, it is not cooperative at all. They deal differently with us depending on the issues at stake, even if the activists or organizations calling for human rights and freedoms are the same as the ones calling for women's empowerment. However, I cannot deny that there are

---

[3] Interview, Amman, July 2018.

important debates going on between civil society actors, the government, and the parliament. These are very important, because without them we cannot advance change.[4]

Different laws have been developed to ensure that civil society is contained, and that the regime maintains hegemony over these actors. For instance, according to the societies and social bodies law, no. 33 of 1966, voluntary associations are to be established by a minimum of seven individuals whose goal is 'to provide social services without any intention of financial gain or any other personal gain, including political gain' (Wiktorowicz 2002, 116). As of 2010, there were almost 5,700 civil society organizations in Jordan, with this figure having seen notable growth after political liberalization measures were introduced in 1989 (Wiktorowicz 2000; Baylouny 2010; Al Urdun Al Jadid Research Center 2010).

NGOs in Jordan are divided into three different interrelated categories: the non-governmental, the 'semi-government', and the 'royal'. All are monitored and regulated according to restrictive laws. Royal NGOs (RONGOs), however, are established by royal decree and are not subject to the laws governing NGOs (Brand 1998). They do not need government permissions for most of their activities and can also apply and receive funds from international donors without official permission (Clark and Michuki 2009). A major criticism of RONGOs from members of ordinary NGOs is that they compete with the grassroots NGOs for funding. One of our informants said that their organization had once applied to a fund from an international organization to promote youth participation. However, the funds went instead to one of the RONGOs, even though our informant's programme would have reached more constituents in several Jordanian governorates. 'People who work in these organizations are just employees who act like bureaucrats. They are not passionate about their goals, whereas we work in this field because we believe in the cause. It is easier for international foundations to fund these RONGOs than us, due to different legal and political requirements'.[5]

Women's Organizations and Activism after the Arab Uprisings

Women's organizations engage in collective action in the Jordanian public sphere and can be involved in a conflictual relationship with social forces at

---

[4] Interview, June 2018.
[5] Interview, July 2018.

certain times and with the regime at other times.[6] Actors belonging to various civil society organizations, such as NGO staff or media personnel, have dense informal networks and share a distinctive collective identity (Della Porta and Diani 2006). Actors in the women's rights movement have been networking since the 1990s to advance women's rights. The political context permitted the development of this movement, mainly through the political liberalization that started in the 1990s and the subsequent opening of spaces for civil society actors. King Hussein and King Abdullah II have been proponents of some women's rights legislation through direct intervention and accommodation of women activists. Nevertheless, Jordan is still considered by other countries in the region to have the most conservative family laws (Benstead 2016), and the conservative and patriarchal voices in Jordanian society are a major obstacle to further progress.

One of the main accomplishments of the women's coalitions is getting a few provisions changed in the penal code, in particular provisions 98/99 and 340. These were the laws pertaining to honour crimes against women, which granted a husband who had perpetrated adultery a reduced sentence and sometimes an 'excuse' for the act. The women's movement was able to push through a change that allowed women who committed the same crime to receive a reduced sentence (Human Rights Watch 2004). The networking and contentious activities of the women's movement have also helped to reform article 72 of the labour law. This reform made it mandatory for organizations to provide childcare centres for women in the workplace (Azzam 2020). These campaigns were conducted prior to the Arab uprisings of 2011.

Since these uprisings, the repertoires of contention of civil society activists have been similar to those of the grassroot activists discussed in Chapter 4. Activists utilize demonstrations, online campaigns, and public awareness campaigns, in addition to reaching out to government and parliamentary representatives to advance new laws. The regime's response towards them varies, depending on their claims. When the claims are aligned with the regime's perception of reform, they are tolerated. However, if they do not align and could pose a security threat, as perceived by the regime, they are repressed through subtle means, which will now be discussed.

---

[6] This section is based on fieldwork conducted with activists in the Jordanian women's movement between July 2018 and January 2019. For more information on the fieldwork, please refer to the 'Introduction'.

Coalition-Building and Networks

Prior to the 2011 uprisings, activists had abstained from participation in formal networks, organizations, and institutions, due to the increase in targeted repression against different activists. Sometimes, the abstention from participation in formal institutions allows activists to remain resistant to an authoritarian regime's co-optation strategies. This helps their capacity to mobilize and decreases the capacity of the regime to repress certain movements and/or organizations. Networks and coalitions become adaptable and are able to collaborate with others on certain topics of interest. This facilitates the development of cross-ideological coalitions, culminating in coalition networks. These networks are contingent on time and space and involve various forms of interaction between different groups and individuals. They also have an ad hoc nature and come together only in isolated campaigns or during certain protest events. Under normal circumstances these coalition networks would not mobilize together; however, sometimes when political opportunities erupt, they cooperate 'temporarily to share resources, frames, and information, to pursue a specific cause that is framed as a common cause' (Berriane and Duboc 2019, 405). According to Durac and Cavatorta (2015), it is precisely due to this fluid and flexible nature that coalitions have the potential and the ability to shift and change existing social structures and boundaries. Coalitions, however, are not all similar in their strategies, especially given that the structure of authoritarianism varies in different authoritarian regime types. According to Schwedler and Clark (2006), activists build different coalition networks based on their objectives. These objectives lead to different cooperation measures, which are basically either low-level, mid-level, or high-level cooperation. Building on these typologies, Kraetzschmar argues that there is a need to look at the objectives of cooperation between different actors and the actors which are involved in these coalitions (Kraetzschmar 2011, 289). The political context is important for our understanding of coalition-building (Clark 2010). Buehler (2018), for instance, argues that coalitions are sometimes able to survive despite ideological variances, while at other times they do not. Thus he states that the mechanisms which are developed by authoritarian regimes to break various alliances also have a lot to do with coalition-building and their impact. Efficiency and access to networks increases the prospects for collective action, and the efficacy of collective action can be partially conditional on the inclusiveness of networks and organizations (Berriane and Duboc 2019).

The Impact of Concessions and Targeted Repression on Women's Rights Coalitions

To enact reforms and changes to advance women's rights, many coalitions have been established by civil society actors. Four of them are examined next. Three were able to advance policy and legal reform, while one was not. The first three are examples of coalition-building for the respective goals of changing the penal code, providing women teachers with the right to receive their salaries via bank transfers, and the provision of daycare facilities in the workplace. These coalitions have demonstrated the ability of civil society actors to form coalitions for social change within the confines of the political and field opportunities available. In these three cases, the regime used targeted repression against certain activists, yet concessions by the regime were the rule rather than the exception. Concessions were prevalent in these cases, since the regime did not perceive the grievances or coalitions as threating to its security. However, the fourth campaign called for Jordanian women who are married to non-Jordanian men to be given the right to pass on their citizenship to their children. This campaign was not successful, and targeted repression against activists in this movement was used by the regime to curtail the movement's demands.

In 2017, the Jordanian parliament voted to abolish article 308 of the penal code, which allowed a rapist to escape punishment if he married his victim (Husseini 2017). This law was changed after years of collaboration and activism by various women's rights advocates, who established a coalition of NGOs working on human rights and women's rights, together with independent activists, to get the article abolished. One of their most effective tactics was networking with the international community. Some NGOs, in particular the Arab Women's Organization send annual reports to the United Nations on the application of laws in Jordan.[7] Their reports to the Committee on the Elimination of Discrimination against Women (CEDAW) made clear the discriminatory nature of article 308 of the penal code. The Jordanian coalition utilized the importance attached by the regime to its international image as a liberalized monarchy to advance a call for this article to be abolished. The reports to CEDAW were perceived as a political opportunity to advance change. According to one interviewee:

> Article 308 changed because there was a political will and need to change it, since there was international pressure to change and the international community was

[7] Interview, July 2018.

watching Jordan's developments in this matter. When you have pressure from the movements and they are networked with the international community, they can pressure the government to change. So he [the king] wants to say that this was a recommendation from the UN to Jordan, and here, we have changed it. An important aspect for the women's movement in Jordan is that when a coalition works to reform something, it cannot only work on reforming the laws from within, but also takes regional and international networking to change.[8]

Activists for this cause not only pressured the regime through international campaigns, but also developed a signature campaign, online petitions, and discussions with parliamentarians to abolish this law (UN Women 2017). While the vote in parliament was taking place, a sit-in mobilized by activists was held in front of the parliament to keep up the pressure (Husseini 2017).

Another coalition, the 'Stand Up for Teachers' campaign, was established to grant female teachers in private schools their right to equal salaries of their male colleagues. It was based on networked partnerships between independent activists, the teachers' union, and independent teachers in private schools. The campaign was started in reaction to a 2013 finding by the International Labour Organization (ILO) about a large discrepancy between male and female teachers' salaries. It began in Irbid, which had the highest salary discrepancy in the country,[9] after a workshop run by an NGO in the city to understand how women felt about this discrepancy and to hear their complaints. A few women attendees said they were afraid to talk about this issue, so they developed a 'core group' consisting of six women who would be in charge of mobilizing for equality of pay in private schools. Some female teachers explained that they did not receive the minimum wage, and sometimes received no salaries at all. Mobilizational structures and repertoires were mainly dependent on sit-ins and demonstrations in front of the Ministry of Education and online campaigns in support of their claim. One important slogan was 'Our Salary in the Bank'. The change in the contract was 'groundbreaking because they could prove when they did receive their salaries and when they did not. Previously they were not able to, so when the administration did not pay salaries, it was not traceable'.[10] Accordingly, they pushed for ensuring that teachers' contracts included that salaries would be paid into bank accounts rather than paid in cash. This became mandatory if women teachers ask for it.

---

[8] Interview, October 2018.
[9] Interview, July 2018.
[10] Ibid.

Another campaign revolved around changing the labour law; women's organizations and feminist activists advocated for childcare centres to be established in the workplace to help increase the percentage of women in the workforce. They built a coalition of six organizations: the Arab Women Organization, the Union for the Jordanian Woman, the Center for Women's Solidarity, Adl Center, Finiq Center, and the Worker' Observatory for Workers' Rights.

> Our goal was to pressure the companies; we did not want to pressure the government, but we wanted to influence companies to cooperate with the Ministry of Labour, and we were able to accomplish this. This was a campaign in which civil society organizations and the government pressured the companies.[11]

This idea also inspired a public opinion campaign which showed that for women to be able to participate in the economy, they needed a supportive environment. 'Some people criticize us for working with the parliament, since it is not legitimate; however, this is the only space that is available to us. You need to work wherever there is a political opening ... you need to use it and eventually other spaces might open.'[12] According to this activist, without the government's support, this campaign would have struggled to be effective.

Lastly, the 'My Citizenship is a Right for My Family' coalition networked among different organizations and activists to change the Jordanian nationality law. In Jordan, this law does not permit the children of non-Jordanian fathers to obtain Jordanian nationality, even if their mothers are Jordanian. The coalition used sit-ins, online campaigns, and coalition partnerships with various activists and civil society actors. Although a change in the law was not achieved, actors in this campaign believed that 'all the sit-ins, publications, and networking with other coalitions changed the perception of society and the state toward us [women married to non-Jordanians]. The idea became a public opinion concern. Discussions with parliamentarians were very important for the movement. Sometimes it was positive and at others negative'.[13]

The parliamentarians were more supportive than the government, yet according to the same interviewee:

> Unfortunately, with the government there was no help ... we met with ministers, but I don't know how to say it so I don't use a wrong term ... we were told that the

---

[11] Interview, July 2018.
[12] Ibid.
[13] Interview, July 2018.

problem is the narrow-mindedness in society ... some of them, for instance, say that they believe in our cause but are afraid of a backlash, or what they call [the power of conservative backlash].[14]

Nevertheless, this law was not changed, and some maintain that that it was because many Jordanian women are married to Palestinians, and the regime does not want to tilt the delicate political balance towards Palestinians.[15] Preventing this is a national security concern for the regime. Hence, there is no political will to advance this change, and the regime works against such activists through subtle forms of repression.

Activists who participated in this campaign told the research team that it raised problems and security concerns and did not resonate with the rest of society because only those directly affected by the lack of citizenship rights formed the core of the campaign. One of their major problems is that they are politically vulnerable and if/when the security apparatus threatens any of their activities, they stop them. According to one activist in this campaign, 'We once had a sit-in, and during the sit-in the police asked a few attendees for their IDs. Even though the security did not detain anyone ... the sit-in was dismantled, because participants were afraid that they would be questioned or that their already precarious situation would become worse.'[16] Here the constraints are manifold, showing how the political and the field opportunities impact the extent to which coalitions can advance change. The constraints here come from both the 'political' and from society more broadly. The regime perceives this topic as a national security issue which might tilt the population dynamics in favour of Palestinians, and the same concern is transmitted to society, who close off the field opportunity of this coalition.

These coalitions show that civil society actors are able to network and use their linkages with state institutions like the government and the parliament to influence change. Reforms like this are only achievable with the regime's consent, but by the same token, could not even be presented without the presence of a strong women's movement in the polity. Nevertheless, while the demand for Jordanian women to be able to transmit their nationality to their children has grown since 2010, the law has not yet been changed.

---

[14] Ibid.
[15] Interview, July 2018.
[16] Interview, Amman, July 2018.

The Concession-Repression Nexus

Activists in these different coalitions argue that they face two main obstacles. The first is the legal environment, with laws limiting freedom of opinion and expression. They particularly pointed out that the cybercrime law and the publication law impede their ability to mobilize for further change. Many activists are afraid to voice dissent or to mobilize for demonstrations and sit-ins because security permissions must be granted for these to take place (Azzam 2018).

Some interviewees argued that the women's networks were not able to bring about the change they wanted:

> In general, we are constrained by restrictive laws, there are regional problems, and since 2013 there has been an increase in laws to restrict the work of various coalitions. There is also a closure of the public sphere by security. Some restrictive rules are written and some are unwritten, yet these unwritten rules are also enforced. One of the major problems today is self-censorship. For instance, in a recent survey of freedom of the press in Jordan, 85 percent of reporters said they self-censor. Unfortunately, I am also included in this. I know my red lines and I work within them.[17]

In only one case, the 'Stand Up for Teachers' coalition, did the regime use targeted repression against women activists. As mentioned previously, three teachers were laid off from their jobs in the private sector because of their activism in creating the coalition.[18] Nevertheless, this repression did not discourage them from continuing their activism.

> Two of them have been without a job for two years; however, they did not leave the coalition, they became the most active people in the mobilization process. Other women faced an online and media defamation and smear campaign against female activists in the coalition. In addition, the security forces do not grant them permission to demonstrate.[19]

According to one activist, 'The school directors are afraid of teachers who have been active in the teachers' coalition. They believe that if you are a woman activist, you are dangerous to the establishment.'[20]

---

[17] Interview, September 2018.
[18] Interview, July 2018.
[19] Interview, Amman, July 2018.
[20] Interview, Amman, July 2018.

The regime utilizes soft forms of repression against some activists in these movements. For instance, one member of the 'My Citizenship is a Right for My Family' movement said that her husband, who is originally from another Arab country, has been living in Jordan since the 1990s with no security issues, but that after the last campaign the authorities did not want to renew his residency card. She is not certain that this is due to her work with the coalition, but speculates that it is. Another tactic of the regime during sit-ins is that the police ask for the participants' identity cards, and this 'scares these citizens away from participating in other demonstrations or sit-ins. This makes people reluctant to participate in any activism, because this has an impact on their future and their family's future in the country. If a parliamentarian is in the field, then the police do not harass ... but if not, they do.'[21]

Similarly, another activist in the women's movement who participated in the 2011 Hirak and has been active ever since, explained that she does not participate as much as she wants to and does not attend many of the events, because she does not want to get into trouble and cause her parents stress.[22] She also argued that the regime uses the women's movement to its advantage. If women activists call for more rights beyond the red lines, the regime turns public opinion against their demands, especially when the rights that they seek are contrary to societal norms. For instance, the regime conducts unofficial campaigns attacking the reputation of women's rights activists by saying that they are 'atheists' or promote 'satanic' ideas. Thus, unless the regime chooses to align with activists on certain reforms, it does not endorse the movement. One informant commented that, 'If the UN endorses a right, or discusses CEDAW at a conference, the regime enacts some minor changes at home to show the international community that it is "reforming"'.[23]

These examples demonstrate that the political context permits certain mobilizational processes which advance social reform and gender equality reforms. For instance, Princess Basma bint Talal, the United Nations (UN) Women's national goodwill ambassador, is a supporter of abolishing article 308. She supports the different women's organizations and their advocacy efforts (UN Women 2017). Thus the movement obtains most of its backing from the political establishment. Accordingly, a majority of contentious activities associated with these social rights and equalities are permitted in the public sphere. The Jordanian regime, which did not foresee a major threat

---

[21] Interview, Amman, July 2018.
[22] Interview, June 2018.
[23] Interview, July 2018.

to its existence and has been upscaling its authoritarian measures during the past decades, relies more on concessions and subtle repression than physical force.

Linkages between Field and Political Opportunity Structures

Gender equality and women's rights are promoted by some authoritarian regimes in order to acquire international legitimacy as 'reformists' and 'modernists'. An interesting dynamic here is the king's direct endorsement of women's rights. After the parliament was dissolved in 2001, the king endorsed new family laws that were 'liberal' and in favour of women's rights and equality, such as the khul' law, which would grant women the right to initiate a divorce. Another law endorsed by the monarchy increased punishments for men who committed honour crimes (Muhtaseb et al. 2016). Yet when a campaign to eliminate honour crimes gathered signatures in 1999 and 2000, seeking to change the penal code to put in place lower sentences for men convicted of these crimes, the regime supported it. Some Jordanian NGOs have been working very closely with the regime to promote the Family Protection Initiative. Another campaign, dating back to the 1990s, was mounted to combat domestic violence. The regime, and especially the monarchy, have tended to endorse these campaigns around reducing violence against women and children. 'These varied initiatives have drawn in external and Jordanian state, non-state and semi-state actors whose overall impact on society is multidimensional and complex' (Watkins 2020, 391). Other NGOs focused on family protection and gender equity work very closely with the government to influence legal change. This camp faced much criticism from conservative and Islamist voices in the country, yet the regime endorsed it (Harmsen 2008). This is part of its survival strategy to retain power and develop more networks with social forces (Watkins 2020). Paradoxically, in order to pursue women's rights and empowerment, civil society actors have to depend on the authoritarian regime that protects them.

The field opportunities constrain some contentious activities, for example the fear of layoffs if employees demonstrate or unionize, as happened to three teachers who lost their jobs. Family and friends also pressure activists against advocating for different rights or demonstrating, or even from posting their thoughts on Facebook. One informant explained that 'I am no longer active on Facebook, since all my family and friends are there. They are very conservative, and they judge me and pressure me when I put my thoughts on women's equality on Facebook. I have therefore turned to Twitter, where the dynamics are different and where they are not present'. Nevertheless, this same activist contends that the government helps women's movements to flourish, even while they impose some security constraints. 'The problem is that the social landscape in Jordan does not help. Even some people who contend that they are pro-women's rights are actually against them and are very conservative. Yet, time is always on our side; we thought that the idea of women's equalities was very far-fetched, but now things have changed; we have a movement, and this movement is moving toward reform and change'.[24]

Islamists in Civil Society

Islamists in Jordan have several different functions in the public sphere. They are part of the dominant political opposition, yet they also engage in economic and social activities and are an important and integral part of professional associations and student unions (Clark 2012). The Muslim Brotherhood, for instance, has been an integral part of the polity since the establishment of the Jordanian state in 1946. It was legally recognized as a charity in 1945 (Dalacoura 2012) under the Emirate of Transjordan ruled by the British. As a charitable and social organization, the Brotherhood continued to work legally in Jordan even during the decades of political turmoil and during periods when the parliament had been dissolved. The Brotherhood also repeatedly supported King Hussein against political opposition, such as nationalist and leftist groups, thereby expanding its presence in different economic and cultural spheres (Dalacoura 2012).

When parliamentary elections were reintroduced in 1989 (they had been banned by King Hussein in 1956), the Brotherhood won twenty-two seats out of eighty, forming the largest parliamentary bloc. When political parties were legalized in 1992, the Islamic Action Front was established with a predominantly Brotherhood membership. The Islamic Action Front was also successful in subsequent elections, winning seventeen seats in the June 2003 elections, for instance. In response, the regime shut down media outlets associated with the Islamists, and in 1993 the restrictive press law was established by royal decree. The regime also limited the activities of professional associations in order to block the influence of Islamists within them. The Islamists were not suppressed by these measures, but the regime also shifted its red lines to neutralize their power and role in society (Brown 2006).

[24] Interview, Amman, June 2018.

Islamist media outlets and newspapers were clamped down upon, and Brotherhood members were banned from leading prayers during Friday sermons in mosques. Islamist linked hospitals, health centres, and educational centres were seized by the regime (Kirdis 2019).

Professional associations have had a strong public presence, especially after laws restricting the press and political parties were enacted following King Abdullah II's accession to power. Islamists have taken the lead in these professional organizations and began to win the internal elections of several of them, including the bar association and the medical association in the 1990s (Larzillière 2010).

Although the Islamist bloc has been faithful in its dealings with the regime and has supported the king's legitimacy, the Islamists have also engaged in networks and cooperation with opposition groups. In 1997, a large rally against the Israel Trade Fair in Amman was mounted by opposition networks under the umbrella of the Committee to Protest the Israeli Trade Fair. In Marj al-Hammam in west Amman, Brotherhood members, the Islamic Action Front, and Islamist personalities participated in these events alongside secular and leftist opposition members (Schwedler 2008). According to one Brotherhood member:

> We are banished from the political processes; the monarchy ensures that the Islamist movement's real weight is not perceived in society. This is a result of the one-vote electoral process, ensuring that the real results of the parliament do not demonstrate the actual size of the movement in society and on the Jordanian street. ... Thus the movement has more influence on public opinion through demonstrating about the problems and threats faced by the society, we push to let the regime change some political stances ... society gives the movement its power.[25]

Relations between the Islamists—mainly the Brotherhood—and the monarchy soured after the Arab uprisings, especially after the Muslim Brotherhood president in Egypt, Mohamed Morsi, was overthrown in 2013 (Körprülü 2017). The Islamists in Jordan, however, have not experienced 'extreme bouts of repression' as have other of branches of the movement in the region. Nevertheless, the authoritarian regime in Jordan has had an impact on the Brotherhood's politicization in the kingdom (Brown 2012). The Brotherhood in Jordan has also been adversely affected by the moves against

---

[25] Interview, Amman, January 2019.

other branches in the region, especially in Egypt, as one of our interviewees explained:

> The regime threatens them that if they do more or have more say in politics, they will face the same fate as those in Egypt. ... Now the Islamist movements are very weak, because international powers, like the US under Trump, for instance, are not in favor of them, and also the regime in Jordan today does not have a positive relationship with the Brotherhood leadership. Nevertheless, in Jordan we do not have the same clashes between the Islamists and the state as in Egypt and the UAE.[26]

International Support for Civil Society and Regime Legitimation

International support for civil society organizations, and NGOs in particular, has grown since the 1990s and early 2000s, as a consequence of the increase in their number and reach in the Jordanian public sphere, and their strengthening and professionalization (Clark and Michuki 2009). International developmental aid is an essential part of the influx of international NGOs and national NGOs. Funding schemes fall within the larger scope of democracy promotion projects endorsed by the European Union and the United States. The funding criteria for regional and national civil society organizations have been to strengthen the role of NGOs in the public sphere and to democratize themselves internally, so that they can effectively democratize the countries in which they function (Herrold 2020; Carapico 2013).

Nevertheless, many scholars have criticized the idea of democracy promotion and have argued that the 'NGOization' of civil society and their professionalization by international donors has added to institutionalizing authoritarianism in the region. The NGOization has rather reduced the chances for democratization, because their focus on capacity building made NGOs 'ill-equipped to mobilize a much broader set of constituencies around the larger goal of regime change' (Schütze 2019, 105). Another problem with international support for civil society actors is that they depoliticize them. They transform political identity and various issues of collective concern into social projects that work in isolation from the general political context in which they live (Jad 2010; Schütze 2019; Teti et al. 2013).

---

[26] Interview, July 2018.

NGOization leads to the transformation of a cause for social change into a project with a plan, a timetable, and a limited budget, which is 'owned' for reporting and used for the purposes of accountability vis-à-vis the funders. This concentration of power might impede the spread of a social movement in continuous need of networking, deliberation, and mobilization, based on daily contact and personal connections.

(Jad 2010, 627)

Although the increase in NGOs was important in bringing in different voices to the fore of public debates, it is believed that the boom in NGOs shifted activists from political causes towards policy-oriented activities and specialization in issue areas 'among the more technically adapt, transnationalized and professionalized' (Clark and Michuki 2009, 331).

The international donors have changed party members and movement activists into professional implementers of international projects who are dependent on the donors and the West, as well as on the Jordanian regime itself for legal and permission reasons. These dynamics have added to the regime's international legitimacy and have created a mutual dependency between external actors who promote democracy on the one hand, and the Jordanian authoritarian regime, which liberalizes the public sphere and grants permissions for civil society actors to work in the public sphere, on the other (Schütze 2019). This also adds to the depoliticization of charity organizations, reducing their influence in the polity (Ryan 2011; Sato 2017). However, these organizations have the capacity to build coalition partnerships and network with other organizations to advance laws or mobilize for social change. It is not the purpose of this book to argue that they are, or are not, able to lead to a process of democratization; rather it is to understand that they undoubtedly influence public policies and laws through different forms of engagement and networking.

Some civil society actors in our sample showed a reluctance to receive foreign funds, to ensure their independence. Some argued that they want to be legitimate in the eyes of their fellow citizens when they campaign for certain rights and to show that their campaigns are home-grown, rather than imposed from abroad. Others try to help the government and/or Royal Non governmental organizations (RONGOs) to receive international funds. For example, one member of a woman's organization explained that they do not accept foreign funding but can act as liaison between foreign funders and the government, since they have budgeting know-how. Nevertheless, on one occasion after a woman's organization had worked closely with the government during the proposal phase, the government decided to partner with the Women's Council (which is part of the executive), rather than with other NGOs. The international funding foundation did not intervene to bring the NGOs into this initiative, but instead accepted the government's decision.[27] These examples demonstrate how international funding institutions can be pragmatic in choosing their partners for advancing certain reforms. They choose the easy way to support change through existing channels, which are not necessarily 'non' governmental in nature, but are easier to navigate and turn to for receiving the necessary permissions for development work.

Conclusion

This chapter demonstrates the complexities within social and political relations, and how they add to the ebb and flow of contentious politics under a resilient authoritarian regime. It also demonstrates how the political and social contexts are both conducive to and restrictive of political opportunities. Like other resilient authoritarian regimes, the Jordanian regime uses some concessions in the form of political liberalization measures to co-opt the majority of civil society actors, mainly those concerned with women's rights issues, development, and charity. Mass violence and coercion against civil society actors are rare, while targeted repression is utilized strategically against certain individual activists. The regime utilizes both subtle and targeted repression against actors to control the public sphere. This can be attributed to the fact that the Jordanian regime has not encountered serious threats to its existence, other than the Black September events discussed in Chapter 4.[28] Since then, co-opting and ensuring that opposition and civil society actors remain dependent on the regime for their survival has been the rule rather than the exception. Civil society, on the other hand, has used the political liberalizations that existed during the first half of the 1990s for its own purposes.

Campaigns for advancing women's rights and equalities should be understood within the larger political context in Jordan. If the regime had not provided a liberalized public sphere, women's activists would not have been able to develop their campaigns, even if the political opportunities in the polity had existed.[29] On the other hand, the regime could not have advanced

[27] Interview, June 2018.
[28] For more discussion of this event, see Chapter 4.
[29] In Egypt, for instance, since 2013 women's organizations have only been able to conduct an anti-harassment campaign, unlike the multitude of campaigns that women activists have conducted in Jordan since 2011. Nevertheless, it is important to note that between 2011 and 2013 many campaigns took place in Egypt, such as the 'Harassmap' and the 'No to Military Trials' campaigns.

these legal changes without the presence of civil society actors who already had a platform, especially the women's rights campaigners. Accordingly, when co-opting civil society, the regime itself is being transformed. Thus an authoritarian regime whose overall power and legitimacy is not highly threatened in society penetrates and influences civil society and is changed as a consequence of civil society's mobilization strategies, and this occurs without widespread coercion and repression. The red lines may shift, and the power and ability of different actors to influence the polity may also increase.

Bibliography

Al Urdun Al Jadid Research Center. 2010. *The Contemporary Jordanian Civil Society: Characteristics, Challenges and Tasks*. Amman.

Alagappa, Muthiah, ed. 2004. *Civil Society and Political Change in Asia: Explanding and Contracting Democratic Space*. Stanford: Stanford University Press.

Ancelovici, Marcos. 2021. 'Conceptualizing the context of collective action: An introduction'. *Social Movement Studies* 20 (2): 125–138.

Azzam, Majid. 2020. '"al-mujtama" al-madany fy al-'urdun mundh 'am 2011'. [civil society in Jordan since 2011] Presentation at the American University in Cairo. Conference on research findings in Egypt and Jordan. 9 February 2020.

Bank, Andre and Oliver Schlumberger. 2004. 'Jordan: Between regime survival and economic reform'. In *Arab Elites: Negotiating the Politics of Change*, by Volker Perthes, 35–60. Boulder: Lynne Rienner.

Baylouny, Anne Marie. 2010. *Privatizing Welfare in the Middle East: Kin Mutual Aid Association in Jordan and Lebanon*. Bloomington and Indianapolis: Indiana University Press.

Benstead, Lindsay. 2016. 'Conceptualizing and measuring patriarchy: The importance of feminist theory'. *POMEPS Studies* 19 (May): 8–12.

Berriane, Yasmine and Marie Duboc. 2019. 'Allying beyond social divides: An introduction to contentious politics and coalitions in the Middle East and North Africa'. *Mediterranean Politics* 24 (4): 399–419.

Brand, Laurie. 1994. *Jordan's Inter-Arab Relations: The Political Economy of Alliance Making*. New York: Columbia Press.

Brand, Laurie. 1998. *Women, the State, and Political Liberalization: Middle Eastern and North African Experiences*. New York: Columbia University Press.

Brown, Nathan. 2006. 'Jordan and its Islamic movement: The limits of inclusion?' *Middle East Series: Democracy and the Rule of Law Project* 74: 1–28. https://carnegieendowment.org/files/cp_74_brown_final.pdf

Brown, Nathan. 2012. *When Victory Is not an Option: Islamist Movements in Arab Politics*. Ithaca, NY: Cornell University Press.

Buehler, Matt. 2018. *Why Alliances Fail: Islamist and Leftist Coalitions in North Africa*. Syracuse: Syriacuse University Press.

Carapico, Sheila. 2013. *Political Aid and Arab Activism*. Cambridge: Cambridge University Press.

Chalcraft, John. 2021. 'Revolutionary weakness in Gramscian perspective: The Arab Middle East and North Africa since 2011'. *Middle East Critique* 30 (1): 87–104.

Clark, Janine. 2010. 'Threats, structures, and resources: Cross-Ideological coalition building in Jordan'. *Comparative Politics* 43 (1): 101–120.

Clark, Janine. 2012. 'Relations between professional associations and the state in Jordan'. In *Civil Society Activism under Authoritarian Rule: A Comparative Perspective*, by Francesco Cavatorta, 154–180. London: Routledge.

Clark, Janine. 2018. *Local Politics in Jordan and Morocco: Strategies of Centralization and Decentralization*. New York: Columbia University Press.

Clark, Janine A. and Wacheke Michuki. 2009. 'Women and NGO professionalisation: A case study of Jordan'. *Development in Practice* 19 (3): 329–339.

Collier, David. 2021. 'Understanding process tracing'. *PS: Political Science and Politics* 44 (4): 823–830.

Crossley, Nick and Marco Diani. 2019. 'Networks and fields'. In *The Wiley Blackwell Companion to Social Movements*, 2nd edn, by David Snow, Sarah Soule, Hanspeter Kriesi, and Holly McCammon, 151–166. New Jersey: John Wiley & Sons Ltd.

Dalacoura, Katerina. 2012. *Islamist Terrorism and Democracy in the Middle East*. Cambridge: Cambridge University Press.

Della Porta, Donatella and Mario Diani. 2006. *Social Movements: An Introduction*, 2nd edn. Malden: Blackwell Publishing.

Donno, Daniela and Anne-Kathrin Kreft. 2019. 'Authoritarian institutions and women's rights'. *Comparative Political Studies* 52 (5): 720–753.

Donno, Daniela, Sara Fox, and Joshua Kaasik. 2021. 'International incentives for women's rights in dictatorships'. *Comparative Politica Studies* 55 (3). 10.1177/00104140211024306.

Durac, Vincent and Francesco Cavatorta. 2015. *Politics and Governance in the Middle East*. London: Bloomsbury Academic.

Gallets, Barbara. 2015. 'Black September and identity construction in Jordan'. *Journal of Georgetown University-Qatar MIddle Eastern Studies Student Association* 2015 (1): DOI: https://doi.org/10.5339/messa.2015.12.

Gervasio, Gennaro and Andrea Teti. 2021(NOT 2020). 'Prelude to the revolution. Independent civic activists in Mubarak's Egypt and the quest for hegemony'. *Journal of North African Studies* 26 (6): 1099–1121.

Harmsen, Egbert. 2008. *Civil Society and Social Work: Muslim Voluntary Welfare Associations in Jordan between Patronage and Empowerment*. Amsterdam: Amsterdam University Press.

Herrold, Catherine. 2020. *Delta Democracy: Pathways to Incremental Civil Revolution in Egypt and Beyond*. New York: Oxford University Press.

Human Rights Watch. 2004. 'Honor crimes under Jordanian Law: The campaign against article 340'. *The Campaign against Article 340*. Accessed February 2022. https://www.hrw.org/reports/2004/jordan0404/4.htm.

Husseini, Rana. 2017. 'In historic vote, House abolishes controversial Article 308'. *The Jordan Times*. 1 August. Accessed December 2021. https://www.jordantimes.com/news/local/historic-vote-house-abolishes-controversial-article-308.

Isleyen, Beste and Nadine Kreitmeyr. 2021. '"Authoritarian neoliberalism" and youth empowerment in Jordan'. *Journal of Intervention and Sattebuilding* 15 (2): 244–263.

Jad, Islah. 2010. 'NGOs: Between buzzwords and social movements'. *Development in Practice* 17 (4-5): 622–629.

Karmel, E. J. and David Linfeld. 2021. 'Jordan's election law: Reinforcing barriers to democracy'. *Middle East Law and Governance* 13 (3): 1–14.

Kirdis, Esen. 2019. 'Similar contexts, different behaviour: Explaining the non-linear moderation and immoderation of Islamic political parties in Jordan, Morocco, Tunisia, and Turkey'. *Politics, Religion & Ideology* 20 (4): 467–483.

Kitchelt, Herbert. 1986. 'Political opportunity structures and political protest: Anti-Nuclear movements in four democracies'. *British Journal of Political Science* 16 (1): 57–85.

Köprülü, Nur. 2017. 'Electoral pluralism, social division and the 2016 parliamentary elections in Jordan'. *Digest of Middle East Studies* 26 (2): 278–298.

Kraetzschmar, Hendrik. 2011. 'Mapping opposition cooperation in the Arab world: From single issue coalitions to transnational networks'. *British Journal of Middle Eastern Studies* 38 (3): 387–302.

Kussumsiri, S. N. and K. W. Jayawardane. 2013. 'Defining Entrepreneurship: Operational Considerations'. National Conference on Technology and Management, Sri Lanka, January.

Larzillière, Pénélope. 2010. 'Organisations professionnelles et mobilisation en contexte coercitif: Le cas jordanien'. *Critique Internationale* 48: 183–204.

Lorch, Jasmine and Bettina Bunk. 2017. 'Using civil society as an authoritarian legitimation strategy: Algeria and Mozambique in comparative perspective'. *Democratization* 24 (6): 987–1005.

Lucas, Russel. 2005. *Institutions and the Politics of Survival in Jordan: Domestic Responses to External Challenges, 1988-2001*. New York: The State University of New York Press.

Lucas, Russell. 2008. 'Side effects of regime building in Jordan: The state and the nation'. *Civil Wars* 10 (3): 281-293.

Lust-Okar, Ellen. 2001. 'The decline of Jordanian political parties: Myth or reality?' *International Journal of Middle East Studies* 33 (4): 545-569.

Muhtaseb, Lamis El, Nathan Brown, and Abdul Wahab Kayyali. 2016. 'Arguing about family law in Jordan: Disconnected spheres?' *International Journal of Middle East Studies* 48: 721-741.

Nevo, Joseph. 2008. 'September 1970 in Jordan: A Civil War?' *Civil Wars* 10 (3): 217-230.

Oudat, Mohamed Ali al and Ayman Alshboul. 2010. 'ïJordan Firstî: Tribalism, nationalism and legitimacy of power in Jordan'. *Intellectual Discourse* 18 (1): 645-696.

Rootes, Chris. 1999. 'Political opportunity structures: Promise, problems and prospects'. *La Lettre de la Maison Française d'Oxford* (Maison Française d'Oxford) 10: 71-93.

Ryan, Curtis. 2004. '"Jordan First": Jordan's Inter-Arab relations and foreign policy under king Abdullah II'. *Arab Studies Quarterly* 26 (3): 43-62.

Ryan, Curtis. 2011. 'Identity politics, reform, and protest in Jordan'. *Studies in Ethnicity and Nationalism* 11 (3): 564-578. https://doi.org/10.1111/j.1754-9469.2011.01135.x

Ryan, Curtis. 2018. *Jordan and the Arab Uprisings: Regime Survival and Politics Beyond the State*. New York: Columbia University Press.

Salameh, Mohammed Torki Bani. 2017. 'Political reform in Jordan'. *World Affairs* 180 (4): 47-78.

Schütze, Benjamin. 2019. *Promoting Democracy, Reinforcing Authoritarianism: US and European Policy in Jordan*. Cambridge: Cambridge University Press.

Schwedler, Jillian. 2003. 'More than a mob: The dynamics of political demonstrations in Jordan'. *Middle East Report* 226 (Spring): 18-23. https://doi.org/10.2307/1559278

Schwedler, Jillian. 2006. *Fairth in Moderation: Islamist Parties in Jordan and Yemen*. New York: Cambridge University Press.

Schwedler, Jillian and Janine Clark. 2006. 'Islamist-leftist cooperation in the Arab World'. *ISIM Review* 18: 10-11.

Schwedler, Jillian. 2012. 'The political geography of protest in neoliberal Jordan'. *Middle East Critique* 21 (3): 259-270.

Schwedler, Jillian. 2022. *Protesting Jordan: Geographies of Power and Dissent*. Stanford: Stanford University Press.

Tansel, Cemal Burak. 2018. 'Reproducing authoritarian neoliberalism in Turkey: Urban governance and state restructuring in the shadow of executive centralization'. *Globalization* 16 (3): 320-335.

Tauber, Lilian. 2019. 'Beyond homogeneity: Redefining social entrepreneurship in authoritarian contexts'. *Journal of Social Entrepreneurship* 12 (1): 50–68.

Teti, Andrea, Darcy Thompson, and Christopher Noble. 2013. 'EU democracy assistance discourse in its new response to a changing neighbourhood'. *Democracy and Security* 9 (1–2): 61–79.

Tarrow, Sydney. 1996. 'Social movements in contentious politics: A review article'. *The American Political Science Review* 90 (4): 874–883.

Tarrow, Sydney. 1998. *Power in Movement: Social Movements and Contentious Politics*. New York: Cambridge University Press.

UN Women. 2017. *Jordanian Parliament abolishes law that allowed rapists to avoid prosecution by marrying their victims.* 4 August. Accessed 7 December 2021. https://www.unwomen.org/en/news/stories/2017/8/news-jordanian-parliament-abolishes-law-that-allowed-rapists-to-avoid-prosecution.

Watkins, Jessica. 2020. 'Combating domestic abuse in Jordan from the top-down: Liberal and/or democratic statebuilding?' *Journal of Intervention and Statebuilding* 14 (3): 389–409.

Wiktorowicz, Quintan. 2000. 'Civil society as social control: State power in Jordan'. *Comparative Politics* 33 (1): 43–61.

Wiktorowicz, Qunitan. 2002. 'The political limits to nongovernmental organizations in Jordan'. *World Development* 30 (1): 77–93.

Yom, Sean. 2009. 'Jordan: Ten more years of autocracy'. *Journal of Democracy* 20 (4): 151–166.

Conclusion

This book answers the question of why authoritarian regimes utilize different repressive strategies towards civil society actors and how these actors respond to these strategies. The book demonstrates that repressive strategies towards civil society actors vary in authoritarian regimes, depending on the regime's recent experience with breakdown and/or continuity. Those regimes which undergo breakdown and transition from one autocratic rule to another increase coercion through widespread repression directed towards all civil society actors, even when they are not in the political opposition. In addition to widespread repression against all civil society actors, targeted repression towards the political opposition is also utilized. This instils fear in both civil society actors and citizens at large. This prompts opposition actors to either disengage from civic and political activism or develop different forms of participatory patterns, like business entrepreneurship. They also develop charity organizations that partner with the regime, in an effort to continue their work with minimal harassment. The rest of civil society actors become more disengaged and individualized, refraining from participation in political or organizational proceedings. This leads to demobilization, at least in the first few years of an authoritarian regime building process.

Conversely, authoritarian regimes that have been resilient to political change and have not faced breakdown utilize less violence and rely on targeted repression and co-optation strategies towards civil society actors. At the same time, they also tolerate different forms of activism and contentious politics. Civil society actors in these regimes are able to use the political opportunities that are prevalent to develop different forms of coalition partnerships and networks to mobilize and advance socioeconomic and political change. In these cases targeted repression diffuses and weakens movements, where large scale mobilization are hard to attain, yet civil society actors are capable of advancing different coalition partnerships and networks for small-scale mobilization and change.

The book adds to the burgeoning literature on the consequences of repression in authoritarian regimes through an analysis of the different types of repressive strategies employed by authoritarian regimes in the same region.

It also adds to the literature on social movements through a nuanced analysis of the consequences of repression on mobilization. This argument is developed through an in-depth analysis of Egypt and Jordan, two countries in the Middle East that have had different experiences in terms of regime breakdown and continuity since the 2010–2011 Arab uprisings. Egypt underwent regime breakdown, with Hosni Mubarak succumbing to popular pressure and ending his thirty-year rule. The military-led regime then embarked on an autocratization process during which coercion, violence, and widespread repression against the public and civil society actors have increased. Jordan, on the other hand, has experienced authoritarian regime endurance. When widespread demonstrations occurred during the wave of Arab uprisings, the regime reacted swiftly through different co-optation strategies, such as changing the government, calling for new parliamentary elections, and calling for constitutional changes (Sika 2017). Since then, the regime's autocratization process has been primarily dependent on targeted repression and co-optation of opposition actors.

This argument is based on comparative historical analysis, whereby mechanisms are studied through observing them at the individual level through empirical evidence (Thelen and Mahoney 2015). To further understand these two cases I also employed process tracing, focusing on the development and unfolding of different events over a certain period of time (Bennett and Checkel 2015; Collier 2021). To understand the extent to which civil society actors respond to different forms of repression, a qualitative analysis of almost 150 civil society actors in Egypt and Jordan was advanced in 2018.

Different Types of Repression in Response to Dissent

Authoritarian regimes respond differently to different forms of dissent (Earl et al. 2003). When responding to dissent, regimes use two different mechanisms; the first is the regime's decision to repress, and the second is the regime's choice of how much repression it will employ. These two mechanisms also depend on the regime's perception of threat from society. For instance, Ritter (2014) asserts that when a regime is stable, it is less likely to use widespread repression. In this situation more targeted repression is employed, decreasing coercion and violence in the public sphere while simultaneously eliminating opposition actors. To assume more resilience, authoritarian regimes rely heavily on different forms of political control, of which targeted repression is essential, since violent and widespread repression is costly. Targeted repression is aimed at certain opposition groups or individuals who widely oppose the regime, or who have the capacity of mobilizing different groups of citizens against the regime. As the 'Introduction' and Chapter 1 demonstrate, this is an important strategy for pre-empting opposition and eliminating all types of activism against a certain authoritarian regime (Demirel-Pegg and Rasler 2017). Stable authoritarian regimes with high capacity are the most likely to utilize targeted repression. Targeting the families of opposition groups, or arresting and detaining opposition actors, are the approaches typically used (Deng and O'Brien 2013; Noakes 2018). Other forms of targeted repression are psychological forms, such as emotionally blackmailing opposition figures and their families (Kevin and Deng 2017). This has been highlighted in the case of Jordan in Chapter 4, through demonstrating how the regime uses different tactics of targeted repression against activists mobilizing against the regime in different contentious events, especially during the Fourth Circle (Dawar Rabe') demonstrations in 2018. Chapters 4 and 5 provide more analysis of the use of targeted repression against different opposition actors through the use of various psychological tools, like 'relational repression' (Kevin and Deng 2017). In this approach, an activist's social ties are targeted to pressure the activist to refrain from opposition activities. This is very clear in the case of Jordan, as shown in Chapter 4, where the regime uses its close ties to tribal elders in the East Bank to pressure younger activists to demobilize.

When a regime's perception of threat increases, it uses widespread repression. This is demonstrated in Chapters 2 and 3 where the case of Egypt is highlighted. The Nasser and al-Sisi regimes are the ones who have employed the highest levels of widespread repression in the polity. Both regimes rose to prominence as a result of a coup d'état, and both want to assert (Nasser) or reassert (Sisi) the military's power, with themselves at the centre of this power. As a result, the regime-building process, like the state-building process, becomes violent, and widespread repression is utilized (Stacher 2020; Springborg 2018). Regimes which have weak state capacities, in the sense that they are not able to penetrate society and implement their political decisions as they would prefer to, or are unable to use their state agencies to make citizens to do what they want (Mann 1984; Hassan et al. 2021), are more prone to use widespread repression. An authoritarian regime which is in the regime-building process is generally a regime that does not have sufficient capacity, and as a result, it resorts to more violence than other authoritarian regimes. The goal of this excessive use of violence is to force citizens to comply and to demobilize any potential opposition. In such regimes, repression can also be utilized against random individuals to deter others from dissent, or to build the consent of other groups towards the regime

(Hassan et al. 2021; Davenport 2015; Ritter and Conrad 2016). To highlight this further, Chapter 2 discusses how the al-Sisi regime has been utilizing widespread repression against all civil society organizations, like charity groups or non-governmental organizations (NGOs), whose work focuses on health and education. Chapter 3 zooms in on the political opposition and on human rights organizations, who face more targeted repression than other civil society actors.

When the stability of a long-standing authoritarian regime is threatened, widespread repression is also utilized (deMeritt 2016). Chapter 4 provides a nuanced analysis of this case in Jordan during the 1970 Black September events and their immediate aftermath. When Palestinian leaders in Jordan were perceived to be plotting a revolution against then King Hussein, widespread repression against all civil society actors ensued. Widespread repression is utilized against a wider number of citizens, without distinguishing whether they are in support of the regime, sympathize with the regime, or are just bystanders during certain contentious events (Hafez 2003; Demirel-Pegg and Rasler 2017; Regan and Henderson 2002).

Reassessing the Repression–Dissent and the Concession–Repression Nexus

The literature on the repression–dissent nexus bundles repression into one sort of repressive category, without distinguishing between the different types of repression and their impact on demobilization. In the 'Introduction' and in Chapter 1, I lay out the theoretical foundations of this distinction. Targeted repression is important in this respect as it pre-empts opposition mobilization (Demirel-Pegg and Rasler 2017). On the other hand, when widespread repression is utilized, especially during certain episodes of contention, an autocratic regime can sometimes be faced with a 'backfire outcome' (Demirel-Pegg and Rasler 2021). This means that the opposition can increase its mobilizational capacity through gaining the sympathy of citizens at large. This book incorporates the distinction between targeted and widespread repression into this nexus to gauge a clearer understanding of the impact of different forms of repression on dissent. In Chapters 2 and 3, where the Egyptian case is analysed, this mechanism is most illustrative. Here a more contextual analysis of the use of widespread repression against all civil society actors is advanced, to understand how this impacts demobilization. The main assertion here is that the regime's perception of threat from civil society actors impacts its widespread repressive strategies. The use of widespread repression is not only prevalent during episodes of contention, when the regime uses violence against protestors and passersby, but is actually present in the everyday life of individuals. The 'Law of Coercive Response' (Davenport 2007, 7), where a regime responds with more violence when faced with increasing threats, is clear. The mechanism here is also important, since the regime instils fear not only in the opposition, but also in society at large, who in response rarely engage civically or politically, or even in contentious activities. Individuals are less likely to risk becoming part of collective action, fearing that they might be targets of repression (Hager and Krakowski 2022).

Targeted repression, on the other hand, is more associated with the concession–repression nexus. This strand of research argues that authoritarian regimes utilize both repression and concessions to deter dissent. Throughout this book, and particularly in Chapters 1, 4, and 5, I demonstrate that the distinction between an authoritarian regime's recent historical experience with breakdown impacts the extent to which widespread versus targeted repression are deployed. Thus when looking at the concession–repression nexus, the analysis is more in line with the literature on targeted repression. Here the authoritarian regime uses targeted repression against certain actors in the opposition while simultaneously co-opting others to deter dissent. Chapters 4 and 5 on Jordan highlight this, showing how the regime utilizes targeted repression towards the political opposition, like some members of the East Bank tribes and members of professional unions who had called for the Fourth Circle demonstrations, while utilizing concessions to tribal elders and to other civil society actors, like women's movements. At the same time, widespread repression from this perspective is costly, and hence, the regime uses other techniques of control to fend off public mobilization. In this case, providing material and political concessions, like access to affordable healthcare and more political liberalization processes, are different forms of concessions (Conrad 2011). These strategies develop into political opportunities for mobilization and contestation, while at the same time they help to contain opposition forces and mass demonstrations.

The Consequences of Different Modes of Repression on Civil Society

This book is not only concerned with when and how an authoritarian regime utilizes widespread and/or targeted repression against civil society actors, but also with understanding how these different repressive strategies impact civil society actors and their ability to advance change. More importantly, the book is concerned with understanding how civil society actors respond to and work within the political context in which they live. The interaction between an individual's motivation to participate in contentious activities and their social structure is important for the analysis of the consequences of repression on mobilization and participation of networks and individuals (Siegel 2011). Citizens have individual motivations to mobilize and to be part of collective action. Under repression, an individual's motivation to participate varies. The more people mobilize and engage, civically and politically, the more likely it is that an individual will decide to participate (Kuran 1991; Siegel 2011). Taking the same mechanism in reverse, when widespread repression occurs and more people decide not to participate, the majority of individuals will decide not to participate either. According to Siegel (2011, 994), 'both the strength and the technology of repression alter expected levels of participation, but conditionally on the network in place'.

Chapters 2 and 3 show the impact of widespread repression on the demobilization of civil society in Egypt. Chapter 3 develops on this through analysing the amalgam of both widespread and targeted repression against politicized civil society actors and by-standards. Since Mubarak's fall in 2011 and the ascendence of the military-backed regime in the aftermath, culminating in al-Sisi's ascendance to power in 2013, all civil society actors have been repressed. Even though repression against the Islamists is most severe, the regime utilizes repression against all civil society actors, irrespective of their ideological background or political motivations. The increasing willingness and capacity to use violence and repression against all civil society actors has hampered these actors' ability to develop effective campaigns promoting the rights of impoverished groups, like the protection of street children, for instance. According to the majority of civil society actors in the fieldwork, their capacity to build coalition partnerships or networks with like-minded organizations has virtually ceased to exist. Many individuals within these organizations have decided to disengage from civic and/or political participation. Many organizations have shut down; others have limited their work, no longer reaching out to as many stakeholders as they used to during the Mubarak era, or in the year following Mubarak's ouster. Civil society actors, however, have navigated different spaces and have developed smaller-scale initiatives, and the majority of actors have moved to small business start-ups and entrepreneurships to move beyond the regime's control. We see that the impact of widespread repression is the 'killing' of civil society and its capacity to survive repression and advance change. In this case, resource deprivation is another problem, since the regime's repression extends to drying out both internal and international funding opportunities. Thus the basis for organization and the sustenance of work is insufficient (Davenport 2015).

The impact of targeted repression against civil society actors is highlighted in Chapters 4 and 5. In the case of today's Jordan, activists are aware of their limitations and red lines and are careful to mobilize within these red lines. Targeted repression and co-optation of civil society actors have allowed room for the development of coalition partnerships and networks, which were essential in attaining some political concessions from the regime, as was the case during the Fourth Circle demonstrations. As shown in Chapter 4, the regime's tactics of targeting certain opposition figures while co-opting others is helpful in demobilizing protest events like the Fourth Circle events, as was the case with the promulgation of some women's rights laws. Chapter 5 highlights how civil society actors in such cases align with the regime at certain times to advance legal or political change; however, they are also able to build their own coalitions from below. The women's movements are an interesting case in point, since according to women activists, they are able to mobilize and call for change as long as they do not infringe on the regime's power. If and when they decide to call for general human rights and freedoms, the regime acts swiftly to curb their mobilizational efforts. The chapter highlights how the Jordanian regime is able to penetrate and influence civil society, and how civil society itself uses the regime's reliance on civil society for advancing some progressive change, like women's rights, to its own advantage.

From Breakdown to Repression and Back Again?

This book sought to shed light on different mechanisms in authoritarian regimes that are situated in the same region. Since the Arab uprisings of 2010–2011, the majority of research on contentious politics has focused on the rising tide of contentious politics in the Middle East and North Africa (MENA) compared to other regions in the world (Weipert-Fenner 2021) and the increase in coercion and violence (Josua and Edel 2021). These phenomena are worthy of further analysis. However, this book advances a more nuanced analysis of why and how regimes use repression against civil society, and what the recent historical experience of different authoritarian regimes tells us about a regime's capacity and willingness to repress. The analysis here demonstrates that widespread repression occurs at certain historical moments when a regime is transitioning from authoritarian breakdown to another form of authoritarian regime. In these regimes, the costs of coercion and repression are less than that of co-optation and concessions, since the regime is trying to build a new consensus in society. The widespread use of repression builds the regime's reputation for ferocity, which is an attempt at building political control. Authoritarian regimes that do not face breakdown, on the other hand, and have been resilient to change even after large-scale mobilization processes, are more likely to utilize targeted repression and hence, violence and coercion are limited in the public sphere. Civil society actors are dynamic and act, react, and disengage from the public sphere depending on the type of repression that is utilized against them. Even though both types of repression are likely to demobilize the public one way, or the other, widespread repression is more likely to 'kill' civil society in the short term. Targeted repression is more likely to 'control' civil society in both the short and long term.

This study, however, does not contend that widespread repression is effective in the long run. When a regime develops its capacity to govern and its ability for political control after breakdown, the reliance on widespread repression can lead to an adverse effect. An economic crisis, in addition to the presence of any political opportunity, can increase dissent, which can lead to large-scale mobilization processes. Thus, even though widespread repression is effective in the short term during an authoritarian regime-building process, it becomes more costly once the regime's capacity to govern and control is established.

Bibliography

Ancelovici, Marcos. 2021. 'Conceptualizing the context of collective action: An introduction'. *Social Movement Studies* 20 (2): 125–138.

Bennett, Andrew, and Jeffrey Checkel. 2015. *Process Tracing: From Metaphor to Analytic Tool*. Cambridge, UK: Cambridge University Press.

Collier, David. 2021. 'Understanding process tracing'. *PS: Political Science and Politics* 44 (4): 823–830.

Conrad, Courtenay. 2011. 'Constrained concessions: Beneficent dictatorial responses to the domestic political opposition'. *International Studies Quarterly* 55: 1167–1187.

Davenport, Christian. 2007. 'State repression and political order'. *Annual Review of Political Science* 10 (1): 1–23.

Davenport, Christian. 2015. *How Social Movements Die: Repression and Demobilization of the Republic of New Africa*. Cambridge, MA: Cambridge University Press.

deMeritt, Jacqueline H. R. 2016. 'The strategic use of state repression and political violence'. *Oxford Research Encyclopedia of Politics* DOI: 10.1093/acrefore/9780190228637.013.32.

Demirel-Pegg, Tijen, and Karen Rasler. 2017. 'Protesters Under the Gun: Under What Conditions do States Manage Backfire Effects Successfully'. *Annual Meeting of the International Studies Association.*

Demirel-Pegg, Tijen and Karen Rasler. 2021. 'The effects of selective and indiscriminate repression on the 2013 Gezi park nonviolent resistance campaign'. *Sociological Perspectives* 64 (1): 58–81.

Deng, Yanhua and Kevin O'Brien. 2013. 'Relational repression in China: Using Social ties to demobilize protesters'. *The China Quarterly* 215: 533–552.

Earl, Jennifer, Sarah A. Soule, and John McCarthy. 2003. 'Protest under fire? Explaining the policing of protest'. *American Sociological Review* 68 (4): 581–606.

Franz, Erica, Andrea Kendall-Taylor, Joseph Wright, and Xu Xu. 2020. 'Personalization of power and repression in dictatorships'. *Journal of Politics* 82 (1): 372–377.

Hager, Anselm and Krzystof Krakowski. 2022. 'Does state repression spark protests? Evidence from secret police surveillance in communist Poland'. *American Political Science Review* 116 (2): 564–579.

Hafez, Mohammed M. 2003. *Why Muslims Rebel: Repression and Resistance in the Islamic World*. Boulder: Lynne Rienner.

Hassan, Mai, Daniel Mattingly, and elizabeth Nugent. 2022. 'Political control'. *Annual Review of Political Science* 25: 155–174.

Josua, Maria and Mirjam Edel. 2021. 'The Arab uprisings and the return of repression'. *Mediterranean Politics* 26 (5): 586–611.

Kuran, Timur. 1991. 'Now out of never: The element of surprise in the East European Revolution of 1989'. *World Politics* 44 (1):7–48.

Levitsky, Steven and Lucan Way. 2015. 'Not just what, but when (and how): Comparative-historical approaches to authoritarian durability'. In *Advances in Comparative-Historical Analysis*, by James Mahoney and Kathleen Thelen. Cambridge: Cambridge University Press, 97–120.

Mann, Michael. 1984. 'The autonomous power of the state: its origins, mechanisms and results'. *European Journal of Sociology* 25 (2): 185–213.

Noakes, Stephen. 2018. 'A disappearing act: The evolution of China's administrative detention system'. *Journal of Chinese Political Science* (23): 199–216.

Regan, Patrick M. and Errol A. Henderson. 2002. 'Democracy, threats and political repression in developing countries: Are democracies internally less violent?' *Third World Quarterly* 23 (1): 119–136.

Ritter, Emily Hencken. 2014. 'Policy disputes, political survival, and the onset and severity of state repression'. *Journal of Conflict Resolution* 58 (1): 143–168.

Ritter, Emily H. and Courtenay Conrad. 2016. 'Preventing and responding to dissent: The observational challenges of state repression'. *American Political Science Review* 110 (1): 85–99.

Siegel, David. 2011. 'When does repression work? Collective action in social networks'. *The Journal of Politics* 73 (4): 933–1010.

Sika, Nadine. 2017. *Youth Activism and Contentious Politics in Egypt: Dynamics of Continuity and Change*. Cambridge: Cambridge University Press.

Springborg, Robert. 2018. *Egypt*. London: Polity.

Stacher, Joshua. 2020. *Watermelon Democracy: Egypt's Turbulant Transition*. Syracuse: Syracuse University Press.

Thelen, Kathrleen and James Mahoney. 2015. 'Comparative-historical analysis in contemporary political science'. In *Advances in Comparative-Historical Analysis*, by James Mahoney and Kathleen Thelen, 3–36. Cambridge: Cambridge University Press.

Weipert-Fenner, Irene. 2021. 'Go local, go global: Studying popular protests in the MENA post-2011'. *Mediterranean Politics* 26 (5): 563–585 DOI: 10.1080/13629395.2021.1889286.

Index

For the benefit of digital users, indexed terms that span two pages (e.g., 52–53) may, on occasion, appear on only one of those pages.

Abdullah II, King of Jordan 21, 100–101, 120, 123–124, 134
Agati, Mohamed 47
Albrecht, Holger 48–49
Allen, Susan Hannah 19–20
al-Majaly, Abd al-Salam 101–102
Ancelovici, Marcos 91, 118–119
Arab Socialist Union (ASU) 47–49
Arab Spring 2, 7, 34, 101–102, 134–135, 143–144, 149–150
   concessions after 102–105
   women's activism after 123–124
Arab Women's Organization 126
art and culture
   censorship 61–62
   detention 53
autocratization 3, 16
   and authoritarian endurance 18, 27
   and democracy 16–17
   and regime breakdown (Egypt) 3, 9–10, 17–18, 27, 29, 34, 35, 44–45, 48, 67, 143–144
   and regime continuity (Jordan) 18, 99–101
Azerbaijan 34

Bayat, Asef 77–78
Belarus
   regime-building and civil society 29–30
   targeted repression 24–25
Boudreau, Vince 23
breakdown regimes 1–2, 67, 143, 147, 149–150
   and autocratization 3, 9–10, 17–18, 27, 29, 34, 35, 44–45, 48, 67, 143–144
   perception of threat 6, 44–45
Burma 23

Cavatorta, Francesco 125
censorship, self-censorship 21, 93
   artists 61–62
   under the Emergency Law 47
   during fieldwork/field trips 65
   reporters 111, 130
Chalcraft, John 26–27
charitable and social organizations (CSOs) 28–29, 31–32, 49
   adaptation to repressive measures 65–67
   censorship 65
   cooperation with the government 64–65
   depoliticization of 136
   Islamist 77–79, 133
   see also human rights organizations; NGOs
China 23–25, 30
citizenship, women's rights 122, 126, 128–129, 131
Clark, Janine 4, 125
coalitions and networking 1–4, 10, 28–32, 44, 51–52, 66–67, 122, 132, 134, 143, 147–149
   concessions 118–119, 126–128
   as a consequence of widespread repression 68, 83–84
   divisions within, and demobilization 76–77, 109
   efficacy and context 125
   and the Fourth Circle demonstrations 105–107
   and the 30 June 'revolution' 54–55
   between NGOs 64–65, 126
   by opposition parties 82, 99–100
   regime 95
   role of external actors 136
   and targeted repression 83–84, 118–119, 129, 130–132
   unions 103
   women's rights 123–124, 126–130, 149
Collier, David 8

Committee on the Elimination of Discrimination against Women (CEDAW) 126, 131
comparative historical analysis (CHA) 7–9, 144
concessions 91, 118–119, 137
  in coalition-building and networking 118–119
  concession-repression nexus 6–7, 92–95, 113, 130–132, 147
  economic and political liberalization 100, 102, 113–114, 118–119, 137
  as a form of control 121–123
  women's rights 121–123, 126–128, 132
conflict-dissent nexus 10–11, 72
  repression of political opposition and demobilization 50–51, 73–74
cooptation 1–2, 32
  in breakdown regimes 26–27, 29, 143–144
  coalition-building and networking 125, 137–138, 149
  incorporation strategies 32
  intelligence and technology 23–24
  Islamist movements 77–78
  in long-established regimes 9–10, 16, 27–28, 31, 36, 143
  under Mubarak 48–50
  and political opposition 96–99, 113–114
corruption 30, 120
  activism against 101–103, 107–108
  self-censorship about 111
cybercrime law 80, 110–111, 130

Darwish, Randa 105
Davenport, Christian 76–77, 87
Demirel-Pegg, Tijen 23–24
demobilization 1–2, 4, 6, 67
  conceptualization 87
  and fear 56
  student activism and unions 80–81
  of the political opposition 72–74, 76–77, 80–87, 143
  use of physical violence 19, 55, 145–146
  use of targeted repression and concessions 91–93, 113–114, 149
  and widespread repression 44–45, 50, 51, 148–149
detention and arrests 19, 24–25, 47, 51–52, 79, 144–145
  of artists 53
  during decolonization 23
  of human rights activists 34, 74–75, 83
  impact on employment 111
  of Islamists 46–47, 79
  of journalists 99–100
  of NGO staff 52, 56–57
  of political opponents 23–25, 46–47, 74, 75, 79, 81–82, 84–85
  pre-emptive repression 24, 75
  widespread repression 46–47
Diani, Marion 3–4
Durac, Vincent 125

Economic Consultive Council (ECC) 119–120
education
  demobilization within universities 80–81
  government-led organizations and partnerships 63–64
  impact of neoliberalization 120–121
  teachers, women's rights activism 127–128, 130
Egypt 1–2, 7, 8, 18, 21, 29, 30–31, 44–45, 49–51, 67
  censorship 47, 61–62, 65
  civil society development 44, 48–49
  coalition-building and networking 30–31, 44, 66–68
  control by government-led organizations 62–64, 67
  cooptation 20–22, 26–27
  demobilization of political activism 72–86
  fear 56–61, 67
  fieldwork in 9
  funding control 44, 51–54, 59, 67
  government-civil society cooperation 64–65
  historical context 45–47
  Islamist movements 77–79
  25 January Uprising 50
  media control 46–47, 50–52, 57, 84
  political opportunities and repression 65–67
  Raba'a Square massacre 54–55, 74–77
  regime breakdown 17–18
  restrictive legislation 47–49, 56–58, 67, 80–81

Index

'terrorism' 35
Tiran and Sanafir controversy 84–86
Egyptian Initiative for Personal Rights (EIPR) 74–75
employment
　cooptation measures 112–113
　labour protests 103, 120–121
　restrictions and loss of 19, 59–60, 111, 112, 132–133
　women's rights 120–121, 127–128, 130
Ethiopia 34

family
　cooptation measures 113
　criticism and pressures against activism 107–108, 132–133
　targeted repression of 24–25, 82, 110–111, 113
　women's rights activism 128–129, 131
fear, and demobilization 1, 6, 46–47, 72, 87, 143, 146–147
　in Egypt 53, 56–61, 67, 76–77, 85–86
　in Jordan 110–111, 129–133
Fourth Circle demonstrations 92, 105–109, 111–114, 144–145, 147, 149
funding 64–66, 82, 87, 135
　concessions to RONGOs 123, 136–137
　and democracy promotion 83–84
　to government-led organizations 62
　lack of 59
　NGO foreign funding law 48, 51–52, 57, 74–75, 83
　restrictions 21, 33–34, 47, 51–54, 56–57, 59, 74–75, 83, 86, 122
　stop, because of political issues 82, 87, 100–101

Gezi Park protests 23–24
Goldstone, Jack 92–93
Greitens, Sheena Chestnut 3

Herrold, Catherine 51–52
Hirak movement 101–108, 112
Holmes, Amy Austin 55
human rights organizations 6, 9, 10–11, 18, 72–74, 87
　control, and the NGO law 56–57
　detention and travel bans 74–75, 83
　internal splits 60
　under Mubarak 44, 48–49
　Western-affiliated, suspicion towards 34
　and women's activism 122, 126
Human Rights Watch 57, 74–75, 80, 124
Hungary 17
Hussein, King of Jordan 21, 93–95, 100, 123–124, 133–134

intelligence-based policing 23–24, 46–47, 57
international actors 6
　as consultants for economic reforms 119–120
　employment restrictions 60
　funding 26, 33–34, 44, 51–52, 62, 64–65, 82, 83–84, 100–101, 122, 123, 135, 136–137, 148–149
　impact on civil society 30, 32–35, 135
　networking with 126
　press restrictions 99–100
International Monetary Fund (IMF) 100–101, 103, 119–120
intimidation 19, 29, 111
Islamic Action Front 97–100, 102, 133–134
Islamist movements 72, 76, 80–81, 148–149
　ideology and cooptation, in Egypt 77–78
　in Jordanian politics 97–100
　repression of, in Egypt 46–47, 73–74, 79
　repression of, in Jordanian civil society 133–135
　violence by 78
　see also Muslim Brotherhood

Jordan 1–2, 6–7, 31, 78, 96–99, 147
　Arab uprisings and concessions after 92, 101–102
　autocratization 18, 99–101
　Black September 92–94, 113–114
　call for reforms 102–105
　coalitions and networking 94–95, 118–137
　concession-repression nexus 130–132
　concessions as a form of control 121–123
　cooptation of political opposition 96–99
　economic reforms for social control 119–121
　fieldwork in 9
　Fourth Circle demonstrations 92, 105–107, 113–114
　internal splits in activism 109
　international support 135–137

Jordan (*Continued*)
   Islamists in 133–135
   repression-concession nexus 93
   societal and economic
      liberalization 99–101
   societal and family criticism of
      activism 107–108
   targeted repression 91, 109–113
   women's activism 122–124, 126–132
Jordanian National Union 94–95

Kifaya movement 30–31, 54–55
Kingsley, Patrick 74
Kraetzschmar, Hendrik 125

Lachapelle, Jean 17–18
laws 2, 21–22, 29, 46–47, 72–73, 118–120, 123, 136
   against civil society 47–49, 84, 85, 123
   cybercrime 80, 110–111, 130
   demonstration/protests 80, 99–100, 102, 110–111
   electoral 97–98, 100–102
   governing NGOs 48, 56–58, 67, 74–75, 83, 122–123
   income tax 104–105, 109
   media/press control 96–97, 99–100, 130, 133–134
   terrorism entity law 57, 67, 80
   vague, as a pre-emptive strategy 121–122
   women's rights 123–124, 126–129, 132, 149
Licht, Amanda 19–20
long-established regimes 1, 3
   authoritarian 'upgrading measures' 28, 31
   targeted repression 24–25, 28–29, 109–110, 113–114
Lukashenko, Alexander 24–25, 29–30

media control 18, 21, 23, 26–27, 122
   in Belarus 30
   cooptation strategies 96–97
   in Egypt 46–47, 50–52, 57, 84
   Islamist 133–134
   restrictive laws 80, 96–97, 99–100, 130, 133–134
   self-censorship 111, 130
   smear campaigns 52, 112–113, 130
   as state propaganda 57, 83, 85, 107, 110–113

   see also social media
memories, impact of violence on 22–23
Misr El Kheir 59, 63–64
Morocco 77–78
Morsi, Mohamed 18, 54–57
Mozambique 23
Mubarak, Hosni 18, 21, 44, 47, 67, 143–144, 148–149
   networking against 31
   ouster, and after 50–55
   targeted repression and cooptation 45, 48–50, 79
Muslim Brotherhood (Egypt) 25–26, 51–52, 54–55, 73–74, 77–78, 80–81
   and the Raba'a Square massacre 74–75
   repression against 46–47, 57, 68, 79
   as 'terrorists' 35
Muslim Brotherhood (Jordan) 101–102, 109
   parliamentary seats 96–97, 133–134
   support of the monarchy 133–135

Nasser, Gamal Abdel 44–48, 79, 145–146
National Alliance in Support of Legitimacy (NASL) 75–77
Nazra for Feminist Studies 60, 74–75
networking *see* coalitions and networking
NGOs 27, 34, 44, 62–63, 118–119
   coalitions and networking 64–65, 126
   and cooptation 48–49
   democratization and depoliticization 135–136
   employment constraints 60
   government-led (GONGOs) 31–32, 62–64, 67
   Islamic 77
   laws 48, 56–58, 67, 74–75, 83, 122–123
   repression of foreign funding 51–54, 83, 122, 136–137
   royal (RONGOs), concessions to 123, 136–137
   and security clearance 59–60
   travel bans 74–75, 83
   women's rights 11, 126, 127, 132
Nugent, Elizabeth 21
politics and political opposition
   call for reforms 102–105, 126–129
   and civil society 25–26
   coalitions, as a pre-emptive strategy 94–95

concessions as a form of control 121–123, 131–132
cooptation 96–99, 113–114
demobilization of activism 72–86
electoral laws 97–98, 100–102
Islamist 74, 133
physical repression 73–74, 93–94
targeted repression 1–4, 6–7, 21, 23–25, 30, 45–47, 51, 72–74, 81–82, 87, 91, 143, 147
tolerance of 48–49, 79
pre-emptive repression 1, 5–6
arrests and detentions 24, 75, 85
fear 85–86
intelligence and technology 23–24
legislation 80, 121–122
physical repression 19
political coalitions 94–95
and targeted repression 24–25, 144–147
vagueness of legislation 121–122
protest movements 1–2, 4, 9, 20, 73–74, 99–100, 134
Arab uprisings 101–102
conflict-dissent nexus 50–51
East Bankers 95–96, 104
Islamist 55, 74, 75
labour 120–121
laws 80, 99–100, 102, 110–111
under Morsi 54–55
under Mubarak 23, 49–50
repression-concession nexus 92–93
student 23, 49–50
Tiran and Sanafir controversy 84–86
in widespread vs. targeted repression 23–25
see also Fourth Circle demonstrations

Raba'a Square massacre 45, 54–55, 60, 72–74, 84
impact on human rights organizations 74–75
and rift among opposition movements 75–76
shooting and detention 74
Rasler, Karen 23–24
repression 1–3, 16
concept of and forms of 5, 19
impact of 5–6
and individual motivation 147–148
institutionalization of 80
not coercive/visible 20–21
perceived 51, 73–74
and reputation-building 20
see also pre-emptive repression; targeted repression; widespread repression
reputation-building 9–10, 16, 20, 35–36, 149–150
resilience, authoritarian 2–3, 7, 91, 137
and cooptation 9–10, 16, 31, 33
targeted repression 143–145, 149–150
Ritter, Emily Hencken 22–23, 144–145
Russia
control strategies 21
repression of political opponents 2, 24–25

Sadat, Anwar 47, 49, 79–81
Saudi Arabia 23–25, 48–49, 72–73
Schwedler, Jillian 125
security forces, constraints and repression 29, 46–47, 49–50, 53–54, 57, 58–60, 63, 66–67, 75, 80–82, 84, 100, 109–113, 129, 130
Shafick, Hesham 75
Siegel, David 147–148
Sisi, Abdel Fattah 21, 67, 74, 145–146, 148–149
NGOs restriction law and fund control 56–57, 62
regime threat perception 55
slogans
Fourth Circle demonstrations 107
'Jordan First' 121
Tiran and Sanafir controversy 84
women's rights 127
smear campaigns against activists 112–113, 130
social media
and demobilization 82, 86, 132–133
mobilization through 105–108
South-East Asia 33
spaces 1, 4, 7
cooperation for 63–64
and Fourth Circle demonstrations 105–106, 109, 110
repression of 58
and women's rights activism 128
student protests
in Burma 23

student protests (*Continued*)
  in Egypt 49–50, 80–81
  and Jordanian Islamists 133
Supreme Council for the Armed Forces (SCAF) 51–52
surveillance 19, 93
  cybercrime law 80
  under Nasser 46–47
  of NGOs 60, 66
  and spaces 110
  targeted repression in China 23–24
Syria 110
  impact of violence on citizens' memories 22–23

Tahya Masr 62–64
Tamarrod campaign 55
targeted repression 1, 3, 5, 19, 137, 143–144, 149–150
  of art and culture 53, 61–62
  in breakdown regimes 18, 21
  against coalition-building and networking 118–121, 125–131, 137
  conceptualization 5–6
  concession-repression nexus 94–95, 130–132, 147
  digital surveillance 23–24
  field opportunity constraints 107–108, 132–133
  forms of 93, 144–145
  impact on demobilization 23–25
  of Islamist movements 79, 133–135
  in long-established regimes 24–25, 28–29, 109–110, 113–114
  against opponents' families 24–25, 82, 110–111, 113
  of political opposition 2, 6–7, 21, 23–25, 44–47, 51, 72, 81–83, 87, 91–92
  as a pre-emptive strategy 23–25, 146–147
  psychological 24–25
  by security forces 111
  against students 23, 80–81
  and threat perception 23–24
  travel bans 56–57, 74–75, 83, 84, 93
  vs. widespread repression 22–24, 146–147
  of women's rights 126–131

see also detention and arrests; laws; media control; NGOs
technology 23–24, 147–148
terrorism, terrorists 20, 100–101
  entity law 57, 67, 80
  repression of, as a threat perception 23–24, 35, 78–79
threat 19, 67
  to activists 82–84, 93, 111, 113, 129
  to Islamists 134–135
  to NGOs, human rights organizations 53, 56–57, 59, 63
  regime's perception 3, 5–6, 8, 21–25, 28, 31, 35–36, 51–52, 55, 56–57, 82, 92, 144–146
Tilly, Charles 92–93
Tiran and Sanafir controversy 45, 68, 72–74, 84
  arrests 84
  chants and slogans 84
  pre-emptive repression 85–86
tolerance 1–2, 92–93
  of civil society actors 27, 44–45, 91
  of Islamist movements 77–78
  of NGOs 48–49, 58
  of regime supporters 21, 31–32
travel bans 56–57, 74–75, 83, 84, 93
Truex, Roru 24
trust/distrust 28, 30–31
  between movements and citizens 108
  towards NGOs 53
Turkey 21, 24

unions 3–4, 9, 25–26, 44, 73–74, 80–81, 93–94, 103, 105–107, 109
  role in the Fourth Circle demonstrations 105–107, 109
  teachers' 112–113, 120–121, 127
universities, demobilization in 80–81
Uzbekistan 34

verbal attacks 34, 93, 111
violence 16, 19, 93
  in breakdown regimes 16–18, 21, 145–146
  and coercion 19–20
  in decolonizing states 23
  domestic, women's rights campaigns 132
  impact on citizens' memories 22–23
  by Islamist movements 78

minimal use of (long-standing regimes) 3, 20, 101–102, 113, 120, 122, 131–132, 137, 143
  against NGOs 34
  against opposition activists 53–55, 73–74, 93, 94–95, 110–111
Volpi, Frédéric 4

welfare provision 32–33, 77
widespread repression 1–3, 16, 44–45, 72
  and fear 56–61, 67
  impact of 6, 23–25, 147–150
  'Law of Coercive Response' 6, 146–147
  in regime-building process 16–18, 23, 27–28, 44, 48, 143, 145–146
  vs. targeted repression 22–24, 146–147
  as a threat to regime stability 22–23, 146
women's rights activism 137–138, 149
  after the Arab uprisings 123–124
  concessions to 126–128, 132
  concessions to as a form of control 122
  constraints, by family and friends 132–133
  targeted repression 129–132
World Bank 119–120
World Trade Organization 119–120
Xu, Xu 23–24